DATE DUE

JUN 07 1996	
UPI 261-2505	PRINTED IN U.S.A.

THE CONSERVATION
OF
BOOKS AND DOCUMENTS

THE CONSERVATION
OF
BOOKS AND DOCUMENTS

By

W. H. LANGWELL, F.R.I.C.

WITH A FOREWORD BY

G. BARRACLOUGH, M.A.
Professor of Medieval History in the University of Liverpool

GREENWOOD PRESS, PUBLISHERS
WESTPORT, CONNECTICUT

Library of Congress Cataloging in Publication Data

Langwell, William Herbert.
    The conservation of books and documents.

    Reprint of the 1957 ed. published by I. Pitman,
London.
    Bibliography: p.
    1. Books—Conservation and restoration.
2. Manuscripts—Conservation and restoration.
3. Paper—Preservation. I. Title.
Z701.L3 1974   025.8'4   73-2640
ISBN 0-8371-6810-4

First published in 1957 by Sir Isaac Pitman & Sons Ltd., London

Reprinted with the permission of Sir Isaac Pitman & Sons Ltd.

Reprinted in 1974 by Greenwood Press,
a division of Williamhouse-Regency Inc.

Library of Congress Catalog Card Number 73-2640

ISBN 0-8371-6810-4

Printed in the United States of America

FOREWORD

THE widespread interest in the records of the past, which has led since 1945 to the establishment of Record Offices in most of the counties and many of the cities and county-boroughs in this country, was due in large degree to the enthusiasm of amateurs. As long ago as 1869 the Historical Manuscripts Commission was established to "inquire as to the existence of unpublished manuscripts in the possession of private persons and institutions, calculated to throw light on the civil, ecclesiastical, literary or scientific history" of Great Britain; and the long series of reports published by the Commission was a major incentive. But after the end of the First World War, it had become evident that the wealth of record material of all categories throughout the length and breadth of the land was such that it was impossible for the Historical Manuscripts Commission alone to report on more than a fraction. Furthermore, although the Commission could report, it had no powers to ensure due and proper preservation; and there was no doubt that records of inestimable importance were being lost on a considerable scale through sheer ignorance and negligence. It was in these circumstances that the movement for the preservation of records, which is so active today, came into existence.

It is no part of my purpose, nor is it perhaps germane to the purposes of this book, to trace step by step the history of this movement. There is no doubt that it owes much to the initiative of Dr. G. H. Fowler, as a result of whose efforts the first County Record Office was set up at Bedford in 1923. These efforts were organized by the establishment in 1934 of the British Records Association, which played a major part in educating public opinion. But a new sense of urgency was given to the movement by the outbreak of war in 1939. First of all, it was immediately evident that there was a great danger of destruction (which, happily, did not materialize on the scale anticipated) as a result of enemy action. Secondly, the salvage drive undoubtedly resulted in a widespread destruction of valuable record materials, and would have had even worse results, if steps had not been taken in time to prevent losses from this cause. To meet this situation a National Register of Archives was instituted, and at the same time a number of counties took active steps to preserve their own local records by setting up County Record Offices on the pattern established some twenty years earlier by Bedford. The result was that by 1945, in spite of the distractions of war, the movement was stronger than at any time in the past.

But the new advances created new problems. If, to begin with, it seemed sufficient to rescue documents from outright destruction, experience soon proved that this was only a first stage, and that more was needed. What of the bundle of deeds rescued from a loft or cellar, mildewed and scarcely legible? What of the parchment deed, so stiff that it could scarcely be unfolded? And, more particularly, what of the almost putrefying masses of paper, which might have lain in a basement, without seeing the light of day, for upwards of a century? Dr. Fowler had defined "the chief enemies of muniments" as "fire, damp, dust, rioters and other vermin." In general terms fire and vermin, and perhaps damp, could be circumvented by fairly obvious routine measures: steel-shelving, fire-proof safes and vaults, air-conditioning, etc. But there were more insidious dangers which could only be combated by more specialized knowledge, and there was not merely the question of prevention but also the question of cure and (where necessary) of repair.

In these circumstances it became evident that, for the adequate preservation of archives, a certain measure of specialized knowledge was necessary. Moreover, since each document was unique and irreplaceable, the devising of satisfactory methods could not be left to experiment and practice, for ill-considered or careless experiment might itself be a cause of destruction of valuable archives. The preservation of archives, in short, was a craft or science, which had to be learnt; and with this consideration in view the Universities of London and Liverpool in 1947 introduced courses in Archive Administration for would-be archivists. The present writer has directed the courses at Liverpool University since their inception, and even in that short time he has had ample opportunity to observe how the scope of the subject has widened and extended, and how, indeed, the horizons of the archivist have changed. What only some ten years ago seemed to be the preserve of the historian and antiquarian has taken on new dimensions, and technical qualifications are required of the practising archivist which were scarcely thought of when Fowler published his handbook, *The Care of County Muniments,* in 1923. Nothing, of course, will displace or dispense with the historian's or antiquarian's enthusiasm for archives, and his belief in their importance and significance as part of our heritage; but the development of modern practice means that this enthusiasm requires supplementation by technical knowledge on a growing scale.

Three main developments have perhaps characterized archive work in the last decade. The first is the realization that the archivist is not concerned only (or, in some people's view, even primarily) with the records of the remote past, but that he also must be vitally interested in current and contemporary documentation, which will constitute the archives of the future, and is already of immediate importance for administrative purposes. This has led to the growth of the branch of the archivist's work usually known as "Record Management," upon which much interest is at present concentrated. Secondly, there are the questions raised by the sheer bulk of modern documentation: questions involving storage space, the elimination of unwanted papers, and the best methods of handling and making accessible the vast archives of modern government. Finally, and closely connected with these technical problems, there has been a growing realization of the interrelationship of archive techniques with other branches of science, and of the degree to which the archivist is dependent upon and can benefit from the work of scientists operating in other fields. It is impossible for the archivist, with his many-sided functions, to amass for himself the technical knowledge which certain branches of his work require; but it is essential that he should secure the co-operation of qualified scientists, who are competent to apply to his particular problems the findings of modern scientific investigation.

It is for this reason that I welcome Mr. Langwell's manual on THE CONSERVATION OF BOOKS AND DOCUMENTS. The substitution of new mechanical processes and new synthetic materials for the older manual processes and the traditional materials of the past has created a series of new problems for those whose concern is the preservation of records of all kinds. The widest-known example of this is probably the short expectation of life—perhaps (e.g. in the case of pulped newsprint) no more than thirty years—of the cheaper mechanically-produced papers marketed for bulk use today. The seriousness of the problems thereby raised, from the point of view of preservation, requires no emphasis. Already in the United States it has been thought wise to treat the documents intended to form the permanent archives of the country with specific preparations designed to increase their mechanical strength and render them more resistant to use and handling. But this—as the reader of the following pages will see—is only one of the problems with which Mr. Langwell deals. For just as changes have taken place in the manufacture of paper, so also has the composition of inks been changed, while the development of synthetic and plastic materials has introduced new types both of bindings and of adhesives. In all these cases, it is important to know the qualities, chemical and mechanical, of the new materials, in order to assess their efficacy; and this information Mr. Langwell provides. The mysteries of lamination, the properties of the microfilm as a medium for record preservation, the durability of typewriting and of the various modern forms of reduplication, all figure in his pages.

As Mr. Langwell rightly insists, the new procedures and materials have come to stay. It is for us to make the best use of them. It may well be true that the processes devised by the producers of medieval manuscripts are unlikely ever to be surpassed; but it does not follow that machine-made materials must necessarily be cheap and inferior. In any case, under modern conditions the materials used in the past are rarely available in quantities adequate for present needs. From these facts we must draw the consequences; one consequence being that special precautions are necessary if our current records are to survive even approximately as well as those of the Middle Ages. But this is a technical question, and it is here that Mr. Langwell's special chemical knowledge of such things as the properties of paper is of the utmost value. Under present-day conditions the archivist, like the librarian, cannot advance without technical knowledge and scientific help. It is this help that Mr. Langwell provides.

Few people, I imagine, would deny that there are dangers in the growing concentration of any profession on mere technique. The main danger, without doubt, is that the means may be mistaken for the end. The proportion of our historical records in need of special treatments is not large, and it would be a pity if their custodians concentrated on the exceptional cases at the expense of the normal. The fascination of technology—not least of all for the amateur—may too easily make it an end in itself; and it will be a sad day if archivists turn into laboratory assistants dressed in white coats and surrounded by glass-stoppered bottles, and if love of records and acquaintance with their history and forms and style and language cease to be the primary qualification of archivists. It is sometimes said that the spate of modern insecticides, far from encouraging horticulture, must make any man despair of growing roses or apples or even humble carrots; and the first reaction of the reader after studying Mr. Langwell's account of the manifold ills to which paper is subject, its instability and capacity for internal breakdown, may be to examine the ten-shilling note in his pocket-book and make sure it has not disintegrated before it could be spent. That is, of course, to exaggerate, and perhaps to make fun of what should be taken seriously. In reality, Mr. Langwell's manual is welcome precisely because it is not alarmist and does not exaggerate. It is welcome because it is written in simple language for the layman with no special chemical knowledge, and places at the disposal of the layman the professional scientist's expert advice. It is welcome because it is brief and businesslike, and provides practical workshop formulas, and does not parade knowledge either to impress or to terrify.

The practising archivist and librarian, and perhaps even the professional bookbinder, will find in Mr. Langwell's book as much as he needs, but no more; and that, in my estimation, is a major virtue in a manual such as this. It would, no doubt, have been easy for Mr. Langwell to write a book twice or thrice this length, and formidably technical. To have done so would have been to defeat his own practical purpose, and would have been more than his subject warranted. His purpose is not—and should not be—to turn the archivist or librarian into a scientific specialist, but to provide him with as much scientific knowledge as he can reasonably use; and this purpose, it seems to me, has been most satisfactorily fulfilled. Though I have no scientific qualifications, I have read and (I think) understood every page, and should feel confident, where need arose, to apply the processes here described, without fearing that I might ruin irreparably—as inexpert scientific applications (such as reagents to strengthen faded writing) have all too often irreparably ruined—a unique and irreplaceable document.

For these reasons, I feel confident that Mr. Langwell's book will serve a useful purpose for all whose business is the preservation of books and documents. Indeed, more than this, I should like to think that this may be the first of a series of similar manuals, in which technical and other questions concerned with the care and use and preservation of records may be discussed and explained. As I indicated earlier, advancing practice has revealed many problems, some of them already urgent, which were imperfectly understood until only a few years ago, and there are many gaps in our knowledge remaining to be filled. It is already obvious, for example, that the traditional methods of record-publication— the calendar, the abstract, the descriptive list, and so on—are too elaborate to cope with the vast bulk of modern (and not so modern) documentation. Or again, it has become clear that the study of diplomatic, or the evolution of documentary form and practice, which was elaborated as a means of classifying and criticizing ancient records, requires adaptation, if it is to be applied effectively to the main classes of documents in our local record offices. The whole question of the application of photography, and in particular of micro-photography, to archives, which is haphazardly treated, requires systematic investigation. The terminology used in records work is in need of clarification. And more needs to be said on a topic lightly, but only obliquely, touched upon by Mr. Langwell: the subject of repair. No doubt others, with greater practical experience, will be able to add to this list of desiderata. Is it too much to hope, therefore, that Mr. Langwell's manual may serve as an example, and that with his book as a starting-point, a series may be built up, in which the whole range of the archivist's work may eventually be re-examined in the light of modern conditions?

In addition to its own peculiar merits, therefore, Mr. Langwell's volume is welcome because it sets a valuable precedent for the future. At a time when scientists and scholars are often said to go their own way, oblivious of what is going on outside their own specialized fields of work, it is refreshing to find co-operation between two distinct professions. In placing science at the service of history, and showing how modern scientific techniques can help us to preserve our records of the past, Mr. Langwell has contributed towards bridging a gap which must be closed if the best results are to be obtained.

G. BARRACLOUGH

PREFACE

As a professional chemist and an amateur bookbinder I have had, on many occasions, to discuss bookbinding technique and similar matters with professional archivists, librarians and bookbinders, all of whom have shown unvarying courtesy and willingness to help. As a result of this exchange of information—for so it naturally became—I realized that, if the chemist was often ignorant of what was common knowledge to the archivist and librarian, the latter were often equally ignorant of current chemical knowledge, especially as regards the natural and unnatural deterioration of the archivist's chief material—paper.

This book is an attempt to repay the archivist's help by offering him a contribution "in kind"; by offering him some of the chemist's common knowledge on the properties of paper and other bookbinding materials, more particularly as regards their permanence. I hope in this way to be as much use to them as they have been to me. The materials and methods described are intended not so much for the trade binder, though he may find something of interest, as for the archivist and librarian who deal mainly with documents and need to bind only a few rather special books.

When cost is important the methods of the trade binder will normally be used but when permanence is the chief criterion some modification of the usual technique may be called for. I hope this book will remove most of the prevailing uncertainties in this field and that those who are responsible for records of all kinds will have fewer misgivings regarding the attitude of their successors to their work.

The data in this book has been drawn from many sources and only to a limited extent from my own work. I should like to acknowledge my indebtedness for such assistance where I have not specifically referred to it in the text. In particular I should like to thank Roger Ellis, Dr. C. H. Thompson and John Dent, without whose encouragement and help this book would never have been started, and Doris Chilman, without whose help it would never have been finished.

I hope readers will be good enough to point out inaccuracies and omissions, of which there must be many in a first edition, so that if a second edition is required these can be corrected.

W. H. L.

Epsom, 1956

CONTENTS

INTRODUCTION

THERE is a widespread suspicion that the decay of craftsmanship will lead to the production of inferior materials and that this will effect paper, the chief material of the archivist. Craftsmanship is not, in fact, decaying; it is being intensified and segregated into specialist groups of jig and tool makers. In effect, most of the skills are being concentrated into few hands and these are employed to produce machines which are essentially duplicators. These machines can and sometimes do produce results at least as good as those produced by the older craftsmen. Because modern industry can produce an abundance of cheap and inferior material and because the prevailing demand is for quantity rather than quality, products inferior to the best hand-made material will always be most readily available and will be used wherever possible.

Unfortunately, this applies with particular force to paper and consequently to the books and documents which are the archivist's chief concern. To assert that old crafts and materials must be revived merely because medieval manuscripts have stood up to normal and sometimes hard use for hundreds of years is to ignore the vast changes that have occurred. Books have a claim to special treatment and, so long as there are books to be bound, the methods used by the medieval craftsmen will be imitated as far as possible within the limitations imposed by modern conditions. Often, however, the old materials are no longer available.

The amazing longevity of archives, such as the Domesday Book, which have survived centuries of rough handling and remain in good condition today suggests that as much as possible of the medieval craft should be kept alive and used. On the other hand, modern materials should also be chosen or adapted to suit the modern craftsman's needs.

There is a widespread fear that many of these old-established crafts will soon be lost to industry. To prevent this, efforts must be made to give the individual craftsman the necessary incentive to use his skill for the common good. The trade unions, in their laudable and generally successful efforts to raise the economic status of the unskilled labourer, have used methods which have been, on the whole, unfavourable to the existence of the highly-skilled worker. The insignificant difference between the wages of the skilled and unskilled offers little incentive to undergo the arduous apprenticeship necessary to produce a good craftsman.

Moreover, the craftsman today is faced with many difficulties, quite apart from the insufficiency of his rewards. Some of these result from the gradual disappearance of many of his traditional materials, the gradual change in the quality of other materials still available, and the appearance of entirely new materials. One object of this book is to encourage the bookbinding craftsman, who is often neither chemist nor physicist, to make the best of existing raw materials. Craftsmanship is not static. Those medieval crafts still in existence owe their survival to a gradual adaptation to changing conditions. A craft will almost certainly die out it if has accepted inferior materials. On the other hand, care and discrimination in the choice of materials, both old and new, will give the craft a reasonable chance to flourish again, albeit in a limited field.

At present, the supply of raw material available to the book-binder and librarian is likely to cause them much embarrassment. Their old traditional materials—alum tawed pig skin, and hand-made rag paper—are usually too expensive to use. What can take their place? Some materials, such as goatskin and good machine-made paper, are still available but have been made by quick modern methods. Are these as good as the old materials and, if not, can they be made so? Finally, there is a flood of newer materials, the so-called plastics of so novel and unusual a character that the archivist either dare not use them or finds them so awkward to adapt to his technique that he avoids them after a brief trial. These are some of the problems upon which this work is intended to throw light in the hope that it may be of assistance in this dilemma.

Present-day materials may be divided into the three categories—

(*a*) Dangerous and not to be used for good work.

(*b*) Doubtful—to be used with caution for the present.

(*c*) Definitely good and sometimes even better than, though different from, any of the traditional materials.

If the hints and suggestions offered here succeed in fitting the materials into these three categories the craftsman will no doubt be encouraged to use his practical experience to make the classification more reliable and extensive.

The case for binding certain books and treating records in such a manner that they would last, under library conditions, for at least five-hundred years rests on the fact that the direction of human progress is not always predictable for more than a few years in advance. The exact significance of this is well exemplified by the course of events in genetics during the last hundred years or so. The work of Abbé Mendel, carried out in 1866 in an obscure corner of the scientific world by an obscure experimenter, and published in an obscure local periodical, has, nevertheless, formed the basis for the modern science of genetics. Yet this vitally important account of his work was overlooked for thirty-four years and was discovered only by a lucky accident in 1900. It is quite conceivable that another discovery of equal importance might be lost, not through the obscurity of the publication but through the impermanence of the paper upon which it was printed.

Research workers usually have to spend time looking through old records and even a modern development, such as industrial chemical research, has roots in the literature of more than a hundred years ago. The reason for the examination of old records is that interesting developments often come before the general public is ready to apply them, and unless they are preserved in a form in which they can be consulted by subsequent workers they may be lost, as nearly happened in the case of Mendel.

Perhaps the most permanent records of the past have been the vellum manuscripts written in iron-gall ink and bound by the medieval binders using the materials of the period—linen thread, starch paste, vellum size and alum tawed pigskin. Since it is not usually possible to predict the future value of any document, book or other record at the time it is published and since it is manifestly impossible to prepare every publication to last five-hundred years, some compromise seems to be essential.

The object of this work is to suggest means for effecting a compromise between the medieval practice of making all books and records as imperishable as possible, and the modern practice of making almost all books and records as cheap as possible, to the extent of disregarding almost completely the requirements of permanence. The compromise does not, in fact, demand a change in the modern practice of cheap mechanical paper-making and binding. It demands that, at a later period, when the value of the publication can be more accurately assessed, a sufficient number of the records shall be treated and bound for reference. In this way a collection of books and documents would be built up, not for use by the general public but reserved for the more serious research worker or investigator. These users would treat it with the same care as is accorded for example sub-standard weights or measures. Under such conditions as these a book should have a long life, assuming that any inherent instability of the paper on which it is printed has been remedied and that reasonably permanent thread, adhesive, covering material and good workmanship are used in rebinding or repairing it.

This, of course, is only one aspect of the problem and its solution. Other means of arriving at the same goal have been proposed and put into practice. In the United States, most of the documents intended to form the archives of the State are treated with plasticized cellulose acetate foil under such conditions of heat and pressure that the paper of the document is superficially impregnated with the melted cellulose acetate. This treatment increases very considerably the mechanical strength of the weakest paper and enables it to withstand normal handling and use for much longer than would be possible with the untreated document.

There can be no doubt about the cheapness and advantages of such a treatment for a document that will be handled by the general public for twenty years or so. There may be less certainty that it will last for as long as the medieval manuscripts and still less certainty that it will be required to last for even fifty years. Nevertheless, the United States Government prefers to take no chances in judging the future value of these archives and it considers the treatment cheap and permanent enough to be used for all the material turned over to the State archivists.

Another method of achieving the same end is to copy the book or document on a reduced scale on microfilm. This procedure may be more expensive than lamination but it diminishes the bulk of the original publication at the cost of the inconvenience of re-magnification and projection for reading. Many archivists believe that not only is microfilm costly from the current servicing point of view but that its capital cost is greater than would at first appear. A bound book is not costly to microfilm since the pages can be turned over quickly and usually little or no flattening is required. With papers it is a different story. A file in use in an office would need much more labour to be employed in passing it before the camera. Each paper must be separated from its neighbour, flattened and then photographed. Experience in America and this country shows that the capital cost of microfilming papers, as distinct from volumes, is very high, probably, for a quantity, as high as the cost of a simple building and steel racking to house the same papers. Furthermore, the legal validity of a microfilm has never been tested. It is extremely doubtful if the Courts would look at a microfilm, and it would be impossible to test for forgery and alteration as can be done with the original. Furthermore, the usual microfilm makes use of a cellulose acetate base, the permanence of which is questioned on chemical grounds by some authorities. Still, it would not be impossible to use a stainless steel ribbon as the base and this should be as permanent as anyone could desire.

In spite of the many advantages of the microfilm, many archivists prefer to preserve certain records as nearly as possible in their original form and, in this case, the microfilm does not fulfil their requirements.

Which methods will survive can only be left to the future, but it seems not unreasonable to predict that no one method will meet all needs and that various methods will each find a limited use in the field to which they are best suited. The methods suggested in this book are designed for the preservation of valuable records in their original form for use under reference-library conditions. They are based on the assumption that the paper on which the records are printed or written is stable to the atmosphere in which it is to be stored or that it can be made so.

In this connexion it is important to know the limitations of accelerated ageing tests, since the period of test under normal conditions is far too long, to be of practical value. This applies equally to all materials used. Doubtless, many of the materials used by the medieval craftsmen, e.g. linen thread, starch, rag paper and animal skins, could be obtained and treated in the same way as for those materials which have lasted hundreds of years and presumably they would be just as durable as these old materials. However, cost and other considerations rule out this as a suitable way of dealing with all printed records it is desired to conserve today. The problem, in short, is to decide whether modern books and records can be made to last as long as medieval ones.

CHAPTER I

EARLY HISTORY OF PAPER-MAKING

PAPER was always regarded as a durable material in the past. Before the industrial era, it was made by slow, hand-operated processes and must always have been comparatively expensive, even when the labour involved in making it was cheap. As books were rare and, therefore, valuable, their owners expected a long life for them. The earliest books were made from papyrus, which is similar in composition to paper and is known to have lasted two to three thousand years under good conditions of storage. Modern paper is often less durable than the old and we may find reasons for this in the developments in paper-making that have taken place through the ages.

The earliest paper known is supposed to have been invented in China by Tsai-Lun about A.D. 105. In the British Museum, there is a piece of paper, taken from the Great Wall of China, which dates from about this time. It quite closely resembles fairly modern hand-made paper in appearance and the torn edge shows a rough hairy texture which suggests that it had not deteriorated mechanically at the time it was torn. This sample must therefore be nearly two thousand years old. Yet modern newsprint has been reputed to lose nearly all its strength in less than five years. What can have happened between these two dates to account for such a difference?

The early Chinese papers were made by stamping or beating hemp rags, ropes, fish nets and linen rags in mortars with water until a smooth paste of fibres was obtained. This paste, diluted to a suitable consistency, was poured on to linen fabric stretched on a wooden framework. When the greater part of the water had filtered through, leaving a thin layer of wet matted fibres on the fabric, the frame with the wet mat on it was allowed to dry in the sun. The mat of fibres was then stripped from the fabric and cut to size and flattened. Later, the linen fabric was replaced by bamboo strips held together by silk threads, giving the first "laid papers." Samples of these papers are still in good condition, some coloured and some almost white.

This process closely resembles the modern "hand-made" technique, the chief difference being in the modern practice of stripping the wet, newly-formed sheet of paper from the mould— the so-called "couching"—in order to economize in the number of moulds in use.

Some seven hundred years later the invention spread from China, moving east to Japan, south to India and west to Arabia. From Arabia it was carried to Baghdad, Egypt and Morocco, reaching Spain (Toledo) during the twelfth century. About this time the Italians learned the process in Palestine and brought it to Italy. From Spain the invention spread to France, Holland, Germany and the rest of Europe. Very soon the Dutch became famous as the makers of the best papers in Europe. It is interesting to note that Fabriano, in Italy, has an unbroken record of paper-making dating from the thirteenth century.

The manufacture of paper in India remained, until comparatively recently, at the same primitive level of its introduction from China. In Japan, on the other hand, the original crude process was progressively improved and perfected so that today some of the most beautiful hand-made papers come from Japan. In the eleventh century China was making paper bank-notes, some of which can be seen today. To handle these strong, soft, silky papers, seven hundred years old, excites admiration for the Chinese craftsmen who produced them.

In 1490, paper-making was started in England by John Tate at Stevenage in Hertfordshire. Soon after this James Whatman achieved renown for his drawing papers: Balston of Maidstone still make paper with Whatman's old watermark. (Incidentally this particular watermark would not be of much use for dating purposes.) The developments about this time were largely in response to the rapid development of printing and the increase in the demands of the printing press. Hand-made paper kept pace with these demands until about 1800 when the paper-making industry must have felt the severe strain of the insatiable appetite of the printing presses.

In the mid-eighteenth century, the "hollander" beating engine had been invented. It replaced the old slow stamping and macerating process in mortars by a rapid and mechanical process and must have given valuable help and renewed vigour to an overstrained industry. About 1800, the paper machine was invented and its use spread rapidly and continuously. Its enormous capacity rivalled that of the printing press and since then the two machines have developed side by side. The modern Fourdrinier can produce paper from a single machine at the rate of 2,000 feet per minute in widths up to about twenty-five feet.

Until the period of machine-made papers, the raw materials used were almost entirely flax (linen) and hemp. Later, cotton and then esparto replaced these materials. Esparto was used principally in Europe where it became and remained much more popular than in the U.S.A. Later still, the various mechanical and chemical wood pulps were introduced. Esparto was first used in 1852 and Tilghmann invented the sulphite pulping process in 1866. The sulphite processes made available the abundant and quickly replaceable pine woods. Today pines and conifers are the largest source of raw material for the paper industry.

THE WATERMARKING OF PAPER

According to Dard Hunter, it may be very difficult to judge the age of paper from an examination of its watermarks only. However, sometimes the watermark may be useful in corroborating the evidence of other criteria. The following brief notes on the history of the watermarking of paper are given with this end in view. Heawood, on the other hand, believes that watermarks can be a valuable guide to the date of a map and estimates the probable maximum error of this method as about ten years in either direction. The question of falsification hardly arises in the normal work of the archivist. In the first place, it is chiefly confined to the counterfeiting of bank-notes and, secondly, only a specialist could be expected to detect a clever forgery. On rare occasions falsely watermarked paper has been prepared and used for the dishonest repair of archives and works of literary value, but the detection of this is likely to be beyond the capacity of the archivist.

Dard Hunter gives some warnings regarding the dating of watermarks. The early watermarks were not always dated and, even when dated, the paper bearing them may have been kept in stock many years before being sold. Paper moulds are comparatively expensive to make and require good and careful craftsmanship; they are therefore not likely to be lightly discarded unless worn out, and well-made moulds have a long life in normal use. Even when dated, an old mould, especially one of an unusual size or shape, may be used for making a modern paper. Watermarks of successful paper-makers have sometimes been copied by less well-known makers. A good example of this kind of rather unscrupulous behaviour occurred with the famous Whatman watermark dated 1731. This was at one time quite openly copied by Continental makers. Old moulds, if in good condition, may have been sold to other papermakers without the old watermark having been removed from the wire.

Slight variations in a watermark have sometimes been given a significance which is not justified, there being many explanations other than those given to account for the differences. For instance, a workman using the mould may damage the wire and make an improvised repair on the spot. The clarity of watermarks depends to some extent on the length of the fibre in the paper. Long-fibred stock generally tends to give an indistinct watermark and sometimes the strength which comes from a long fibre is deliberately sacrificed to produce a clear watermark. With these warnings, the historical notes which follow may be of some use in determining the date of manufacture, the composition and the manufacturer of paper.

Watermarking only became general about the middle of the

fifteenth century and the simple forms then in vogue were continued into the latter part of the eighteenth century. Watermarks fall broadly into four classes—

The first and earliest class were simple and consisted of crosses, ovals, circles, knots, triangles, three hill symbols and similar devices that could easily be made by twisting and bending wire. During this period many pommé crosses were used; these were based on the Greek cross with balls or circles at each end of the cross bars. Another similar mark found on fourteenth century Italian paper consists of a circle surmounted by a patriarchal or papal cross. This period extended approximately from 1282 to 1425.

Second class. These marks consist of figures of man and the works of man. Thousands of designs of this kind are known, many of them of hands in various forms.

Third class. These include flowers, trees, vegetables, grain, plants and fruits. Occasionally, combination figures from this class and the preceding one will be found.

Fourth class. These include wild, domesticated and legendary animals. More recent developments have resulted in complicated and sometimes artistic forms, reflecting an increasing skill in manufacture. "Light and shade" watermarks, invented by an Englishman named Smith, occur occasionally after the nineteenth century, but they are not common because they are difficult and expensive to make.

CHAPTER 2

MODERN PAPER

INCREASED mechanization in the paper-making industry has resulted in prodigious increases in output and this, in its turn, has completely outstripped the previously recognized supplies of raw material—cotton rags, hemp waste, etc. During the last one hundred and fifty years additional sources of supply have been sought, and now it is probably true to say that no corner of the world has been left unexplored in this search for suitable fibrous raw material. So long as purely mechanical means of preparation were used the available range of suitable raw materials was limited.

With the advent of chemical methods of preparation almost any vegetable fibrous material could be pressed into service and the matter then resolved itself into one of price and quality. In simple terms this meant that the almost inexhaustible supply of straws, grasses and timbers would be at the disposal of the paper-maker. When it is remembered that most of the civilized world is fed on grasses—wheat, rice, oats, etc.—and that timber of one kind or another will flourish on almost any kind of land unsuited to arable crops, it will be realized that both cultivated and un-cultivated land could provide its quota. There are, in fact, very few parts of the land surface of the globe which are devoid of potential interest to the paper-maker.

For the present, therefore, the chemist and the engineer have solved the problem of the supply of abundant and cheap paper. What does this mean in terms of quality? The following notes, which have been epitomized from Clapperton, will perhaps give some of the answers to this question.

The mechanical strength of paper depends largely on the length and strength of the individual fibres. Length of fibre is important since short fibres cannot be made to interlock so completely as the longer and more flexible fibres. Quality depends largely on the nature of the fibres. Some fibres respond to treatment in the beater better than others; some readily become gelatinous by beating and tend to give hard rattly papers. Others readily fray out at the ends and these frayed ends give an excellent interlocking action and lead to strong tough papers. The practical importance to the archivist of fibre length is well illustrated in the case of the so-called manilla folders so much used for office records. The best quality folders consist of thin board made from virgin manilla hemp or from old manilla hemp cordage. But this material is expensive and cheaper imitations containing shorter fibred material and sometimes mechanical wood pulp are very common. The difference in useful life between the genuine manilla and the substitute is often so great as to leave little room for doubt that the substitute is much more expensive to use. The difference is usually most marked when the materials are scored for bending— the substitutes often break through the cut the first time they are bent.

FIBRES USED FOR MODERN PAPER

The chief fibres in use today are cotton, flax (linen), hemp, esparto, straw and wood. In the raw state all except cotton are impure forms of cellulose, usually lignocelluloses, and need some form of chemical treatment to liberate the fibre in the form most suitable for making a good quality paper. All the natural fibres are tubes, often collapsed to flat ribbons, and the thickness of the walls of the tube is of great importance to the paper-maker.

Cotton

The cotton fibre is about 25 mm. long by about 0·025 mm. thick. It consists of a flattened tube with thin walls and is twisted into a corkscrew-like shape. Paper made from it is soft, flexible and bulky. The fibres do not normally pack together very closely but, owing to their corkscrew form, they can interlock and give strength to the paper made from them. The cotton fibre is a very adaptable fibre and much sought after for making good-quality paper.

Flax

This is a bast fibre, i.e. one from the inner bark of the plant. It is about 25 mm. long by about 0·02 mm. thick. It is therefore thinner than the cotton fibre and its tube has thicker walls. It is stiffer and stronger than cotton, has a rounded section and is knotted at intervals along its length. Linen was used by the Chinese for the first paper to be made in A.D. 105. It is used today for thin tissues and cigarette papers but not much for other kinds of paper.

Hemp

Several kinds of hemp are used. Many of them come from waste rope and cordage, some from crops grown specially for paper-making. The fibre is similar to flax and consists of thick walled tubes. It is used chiefly for thin opaque papers with great strength.

Esparto or Alpha Grass

This harsh tough grass grows in North Africa and Southern Spain. The fibres are fine, cylindrical and smooth, 1·5 mm. long by 0·012 mm. thick. They are too short to impart much strength to paper made from them which is silky, bulky and has a good uniform surface. It is much in demand in this country for making printing papers but is not much used in the U.S.A., probably because of the high freight charges that would be incurred in transporting it.

Straw

Straw fibre is somewhat similar to, but rather shorter than, that from esparto. It was not much used in England owing to the high cost of collection and uncertain supply of straws. It is much more popular in Holland for cheap paper and straw board because its collection has been well organized. The Second World War cut off the supply of esparto to England, and straw had then to be used. Since that time esparto has again become freely available and paper-makers have turned from straw, which is rather more troublesome to process, to the esparto for which their plant was originally designed.

Wood

The fibres of wood are of two very different kinds, depending upon the method used for pulping. For mechanical wood pulp the logs of timber are simply ground to powder on grindstones liberally supplied with water. The fibre is short and brittle and is

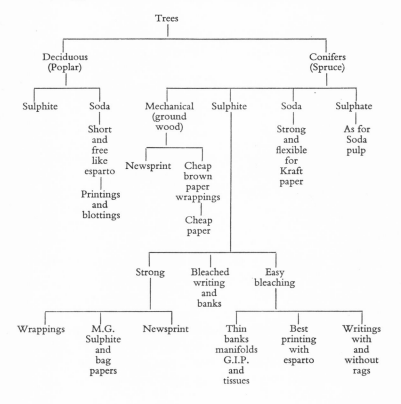

only used for the cheapest papers. Newsprint consists largely of this fibre but it needs a certain addition of chemical wood pulp to give it even the limited strength required for a newspaper. Chemical wood pulps have fairly long fibres, though much shorter than those of cotton or linen, and are smooth and silky. The conifers—spruces and pines—give a rather longer and stronger fibre than that from the deciduous trees—poplar and beech. The three processes used in the chemical pulping of woods are known as the sulphite, soda and sulphate processes. These fibres between them supply the larger part of the raw material for the modern paper mill. Some idea of their versatility can be gained from the table on page 9 which shows the various kinds of paper for which the different wood pulps are used. It also shows clearly the great versatility of sulphite pulp from spruce.

MODERN MANUFACTURING PROCESSES

The highly complex machinery of the modern paper-mill makes any short description of it almost useless. The most that can be attempted here is a short summary which will enable the archivist or other paper user to appreciate the effect of modern manufacturing methods on the permanence of modern paper.

Preparation of the Fibrous Pulp

The old method used before the introduction of chemical pulping was to start with some fairly clean fibrous material, such as linen or cotton rags or old cordage, and to macerate it in mortars by stamping until a smooth paste was obtained. Metal was not often used for this part of the treatment in the early period. The modern method, except for mechanical wood pulp, is almost always chemical and consists in digesting the raw material in large boilers under pressure, with calcium bisulphite for the sulphite process, caustic soda for the soda process and a complicated mixture of caustic alkalis for the sulphate process. These methods free the cellulose fibre from impurities and encrusting matter (lignin) very effectively and cheaply.

Beating

The fibrous material is diluted with water to a suitable degree and given some kind of mechanical rubbing or attrition in order to swell and cut the fibres so that they are the right length and have the right kind of surface for the grade of paper to be made. In the pre-machine era this was done during the stamping and maceration of the fibrous raw material. It must have been a very rough and ready process since it would not always have been possible to separate the two operations of breaking down the aggregates of fibres and the beating of the freed fibres.

The modern beater is a very adaptable machine. It is fed with clean fibres which means it has not much to do in separating out the individual fibres and can therefore be made to concentrate on the purely beating operation. This it does with marvellous precision and regularity and, subject to the innate character of the fibres, it can produce an amazing range of results. The modern beater is generally constructed of iron and steel and, consequently, is liable to add small amounts of iron to the pulp in process, which the old stamps did not do. This small addition of iron may have some influence on the durability of paper exposed to an impure atmosphere.

To the beater are added the sizing materials and any others, such as loading materials, which can be retained by the freely floating fibres. The old "hand-made" papers were not usually loaded, but modern papers often are loaded to give them some surface characteristic, such as increased smoothness to take a better impression from type or half-tone blocks.

The old papers were sized with gelatine or glue mixed with alum and this "tub" sizing was done after the paper was dried. The modern "engine" sizing is carried out by adding a mixture of resin, soap and alum to the stock in the beater. For special purposes, the machine-made papers are tub sized in much the same way as the old papers but the operation is carried out mechanically. The tub sizing bath is rather acid because of its content of alum. Consequently, it is not allowed to be in contact with iron and must be used in a copper bath. This may add appreciable amounts of copper to the sized paper and affect the permanence of the paper in the same way as the iron impurity previously mentioned. The gelatine size, unlike the rosin size, strengthens the paper quite appreciably and both make the paper much more non-absorbent.

Sheeting

The prepared pulp from the beater is diluted to the correct consistency to suit the paper machine and to produce the thickness of finished paper required. It would be impossible to describe in a few words the amazing complexity of this modern giant of the mechanical world or the equally amazing ingenuity of the people who keep it running. It imitates more or less closely the technique of the old craftsman with his hand mould but turns out vast quantities of paper with a regularity quite impossible with any hand process.

Provided the materials supplied to the machine are equal in quality to those used in hand processes machine-made paper will be as good as, though slightly different from, the hand-made product. The machine-made sheet is much smoother and more even than a hand-made sheet and also has a much more pronounced grain. Consequently, the tensile strength of machine-made paper is higher in the machine direction than at right angles to it, due to the fact that the machine cannot give the pulp the same double shake that the hand worker can give during the draining of the wet mat of fibres on the wire. This is important to bear in mind when binding books made from modern machine-made papers.

COMPOSITION OF PAPER AND ITS EFFECT
ON DURABILITY

Paper forms such an essential part of records and archives, that if its permanence is of a low order it is useless to trouble about other materials. A good hand-made paper, made from first quality rags and tub sized, is believed to be almost as permanent as vellum. The permanence of cheaper and more readily obtainable paper is discussed and assessed in the Report of the Library Association of *The Durability of Paper* (September, 1930). But this report ignores the fact that many documents and books will be printed or written on so-called unstable paper for many years to come, partly because the importance of many documents does not become obvious until some time after they have been published and read by the public. How are such documents to be preserved? In other words can an unstable paper be given sufficient stability to last for five hundred years or more without demanding expensive and specially favourable storage conditions?

Before deciding this question it is important to understand the causes underlying the mechanical breakdown of paper, since a chemical breakdown will always manifest itself as a mechanical weakness and paper is only interesting in so far as it is strong enough to be handled. The soundest approach to this question is from the aspect of the chemical structure of cellulose, the essential basis of good paper and a major constituent of all normal papers.

Cotton hair is perhaps the purest natural form of cellulose and, as it is typical of other true celluloses, it will be considered at greater length. The cotton hair, which is a few inches long and thick enough to be seen by the naked eye, is a compound structure built up of fibrils of similar proportion but much smaller than itself. These individual fibrils are only visible under the microscope. They are minute replicas of the cotton hair and are very long in relation to their thickness. They, in their turn, can be shown to consist of still smaller sub-microscopic fibre-like units. This process of subdivision could probably be carried on, at least in theory, until one arrives at the cellulose molecule itself which is too small to be rendered visible by any means at our disposal today. It is believed that even at this stage of subdivision the molecule is a long slender structure very much like the parent cotton hair in proportions.

It is this molecule we have to consider. In the first place, if it is subdivided any farther, e.g. broken in half, it becomes something which in principle at least is chemically different. Up to and including the molecular state subdivision is purely mechanical;

beyond this it becomes chemical and consequently more deep seated.

A great deal of research has been directed towards the better understanding of these molecular breakdowns, since the mechanical strength and permanence of paper and many textiles depend on the length of the cellulose molecule.

Recent work has shown fairly convincingly that the cellulose molecule is built up of very simple units—300–1,000 of them—in the form of a long thin structure like a chain. In fact, it is often referred to by chemists as a chain molecule. Each of the links of the chain consists of a slightly modified form of the common sugar glucose. A good mental picture of the kind of substance cellulose is can be obtained by imagining the glucose molecule as being like a chain link but not closed ⊂⊃ and the cellulose molecule a chain of links ⊂⊃⊂⊃⊂⊃⊂⊂ closed except for the end link. Destructive agents can weaken and open the individual links of the chain, causing it to break up into smaller lengths. The mechanical strength of any aggregate of cellulose fibres, such as paper, falls in response to the reduction in chain length. If the process continues to its conclusion one would be left with nothing but glucose, a soluble non-fibrous substance completely useless as a sheet-forming material.

Such, in hypothesis, is the nature of the chemical breakdown of paper. If one could list all the natural processes which could weaken the bond between individual links of the cellulose chain it would be the first stage in finding the remedies. Since the value of textiles and paper is vitally dependent on this chain length of the cellulose molecule, and since huge sums of money are involved, it would be natural to expect that a great deal of research has been directed to problems such as this. A great deal is, in fact, already known of the influences which cause a weakening of the bond between the links of the cellulose chain. For the present short description these influences may be classified as follows—

(i) Slow oxidation by contact with the oxygen in the air.

(ii) Slow internal breakdown due to acids either in the cellulose or introduced during manufacture or during use, e.g. the effects due to traces of catalytic metals such as iron, copper and manganese in the paper in conjunction with sulphur dioxide in the atmosphere.

(iii) Breakdown due to ultra-violet light and damage traceable to micro-organisms, such as bacteria and moulds.

This may seem to be a formidable array of dangers to which archives are liable but the incidence of most of them is small and in some cases quite simple precautions would obviate most of the risk.

For example, ultra-violet light damage is likely to be serious only under abnormal conditions of storage. Many libraries and archive storage places are deficient in visible light and even more so in ultra-violet light, and even when records are stored under such abnormal conditions that ultra-violet light damage is probable, a cheap straw-board box or container would be sufficient to protect the book or record for many years. Such a container would bear the brunt of the ultra-violet light action and might have to be replaced from time to time. The action of bacteria and moulds is confined to paper which is much damper than it should be and the obvious remedy is to avoid a damp atmosphere. Another, but less satisfactory, method is to spray or fumigate the book or document with an antiseptic. This will be described more fully later. In any case, it would be most unwise to store valuable documents, etc., where they would be exposed either to unscreened ultra-violet light or to excessive damp.

Other destructive agents are not so easily avoided. They affect most libraries and in consequence call for a much more careful survey, examination and treatment, usually of the paper itself. For example, the action of sulphur dioxide in the atmosphere of towns can be avoided in much the same way as it is for modern bookbinding leather.

The slow action of the oxygen of the air on cellulose is not important with sound paper, except under very alkaline conditions which are not likely to be met with in manufactured paper. However, the indiscriminate use of adhesives of unknown composition may be responsible for the introduction of unexpected concentrations of alkali where these adhesives have been used. The use of strawboard, which may be alkaline if badly manufactured, could conceivably introduce sufficient alkali to affect the colour of paper, linen, etc., in contact with it.

THE DANGERS OF ACID

Under normal conditions and using well-manufactured bookbinding materials, the trouble most likely to be met with is free acid in the paper and the binding materials. How serious this can be will be realized by a simple experiment. A drop of dilute 1 per cent hydrochloric or sulphuric acid allowed to fall and dry on a sheet of paper will, in a few hours, cause the place it dampened to become so brittle that a touch will usually cause it to break away and leave a hole. Still weaker acids may have a similar effect, though they may require a longer time to manifest it. Ultimately, the inevitable brittleness will develop and the paper will fall to pieces under mechanical stress. This action is the same as that which takes place in a sulphury atmosphere. In both cases, the effect of the acid is to weaken the holding power of the individual links of the cellulose chain, which then breaks into fragments with consequent loss of strength in the cellulose fibres. Acids are used in many paper-manufacturing processes and it is so difficult to remove them completely by washing that small amounts are often present in the paper.

Apart from these incidental introductions of acid, the purest cellulose known to the chemist is itself distinctly acid, though it is improbable that it carries the seeds of its own destruction. However, it does raise the question, not wholly academic, of the best acidity for paper which has to last. Until this question and the equally difficult one of measuring acidity in paper have been answered, it is quite safe to accept the acidity of pure normal cellulose as a guide since this material is known by experience to be sufficiently durable to satisfy most practical requirements. This question of reaction of paper is by no means a simple one. If the paper is either markedly alkaline or acid the links in the cellulose chain have their grip on each other weakened and the chain more or less readily breaks into fragments; it is essential therefore that the reaction of the paper be between these two limits, with perhaps a tendency to the acid side of neutral.

It is interesting to reflect that most woods are extremely stable materials in contact with the atmosphere when dry. Yet when ground to powder, as is done for mechanical wood pulp, and made into newsprint, they are currently believed to be unstable. The reason is not easily understood, even when allowance has been made for the different states of subdivision of the two materials, but it is probable that with newsprint mechanical durability and permanence have been confused.

Further examination of old samples of paper increasingly emphasizes the importance of acids in the destruction of paper with age. If all possible sources of acids are taken into account it may well be possible to explain most of the cases of brittleness which occur among old papers. One striking anomaly was presented by a newspaper of 1916 (35 years old) which seemed to have retained all its original strength, as shown by a simple but severe creasing test carried out by doubling a sample *across* the grain and pressing flat between the fingers, opening out and folding in the reverse direction, and continuing until the paper shows a break at the crease. Brittle paper succumbs to this simple practical test. It is, however, only a very rough test and is open to so many practical objections on the score of reproducibility that it cannot be used quantitatively without the introduction of many refinements. Usually, a very much damaged paper will crack visibly after the first creasing while sound paper—even newsprint —will stand up to thirty or forty double creases without falling apart. It is a practical common-sense test and should not be made to exceed its limitations. In particular, it should be used with great caution for thick papers and thin boards.

There can be no doubt that acids destroy the cellulose of paper: this has many times been demonstrated, especially with cotton and linen textiles. Even such a weak acid as acetic can occasion a very slight but still measurable weakening and stronger acids are correspondingly more active, so that any treatment which has for its object the stabilization of paper must consider the question of acidity. The sources of acidity of paper are either intrinsic or extrinsic. The acid may be present in the material of which the paper is made and may be left intentionally in the finished paper, e.g. alum used for sizing; the acid may be introduced during manufacture and not be sufficiently removed, or the acid may gain access to the paper during storage and use.

It is important to realize at the outset what is implied by acidity in this connexion. The term has unfortunately been used to signify two distinct things, *intensity* and *quantity*. The chemist understands the distinction and it is important that the difference shall be clear if confusion is to be avoided. The *quantity* of acid in any material can be estimated, usually with considerable precision, by measuring the amount of alkali of known composition which is needed to neutralize the acid of a known weight of the sample. For the present purpose, water-soluble acidity is what matters and in practice a definite and known weight of the sample of paper is extracted with distilled water which is then treated with a measured amount of alkali until the solution is neither acid nor alkaline. There is usually no need to know just what the acid is: the result can be and often is expressed as equivalent to some known standard. The amount of acidity measured in this way is less significant than its intensity.

The *intensity* of the acidity is usually given in the form of the hydrogen-ion concentration, or pH as it is written in chemical symbols. The pH value is a convenient practical form for this intensity and is normally used in practical work. It can be estimated by the colour change which the sample or a water extract of it causes in certain colouring matters. Litmus is perhaps the oldest and best known colouring matter but many synthetic dyestuffs are now available, showing definite colour changes corresponding to definite hydrogen-ion concentrations. These are easy to use and give an invaluable rough indication. For more precise work electrometric methods are used, but these are not usually available outside the specialist laboratory.

The pH scale is somewhat difficult to justify to the layman since it seems arbitrary but its use is accepted by chemists. On this scale a value of 7 denotes neutrality; smaller values represent increasingly intense acidity while larger values, up to a limit of 14, represent increasing alkalinity. Only the acid range is interesting in the present connexion and in practice only a small part of this range. Since this scale is logarithmic the increase in acidity shown by the range 7 to 6 is only one-tenth of that shown by the range of 6 to 5. This applies right up the scale. Thus, pH 3 represents a very high acidity and is not likely to be met with in paper. The interesting range is pH 5 to pH 3; pH 5 is the acidity of the purest cellulose known to the chemist while a pH of 3 would only rarely be shown by paper.

The simplest and most practical way of measuring the pH of white paper is to put a drop of an indicator on to air-dry paper and allow it to dry in the air. In this way the acidity of the paper in its normal usable condition is given approximately by the final colour of the spot on the paper (*see* p. 20). Thus determined, one cannot expect to find paper less acid than pH 5 unless an alkali has been added to it. Ordinary newsprint shows an acidity of pH 4 which may rise to pH 3·8.

CHAPTER 3

CAUSES OF DAMAGE TO PAPER

MODERN processes of paper manufacture are usually too rigidly controlled to allow bleach residues to remain in the finished paper, as was once the case. In the early nineteenth century, there were many complaints about the brittleness of paper which was caused by excessive bleaching by chlorine and hypochlorites. Chlorine was beginning to be manufactured very cheaply about this time and the difficulty of ridding paper of excess chlorine was either not understood or was ignored. Many of these chlorine residues break down slowly, giving rise to hydrochloric acid, the arch-enemy of paper. Excess residual acids are, however, still likely to occur since alum—a strongly acid substance—is almost universally used by the paper-maker for almost all grades of paper and it has many uses in the paper mill for overcoming practical manufacturing difficulties.

It would be difficult to lay down any hard and fast rules as to the safe limit for the acidity of paper and the only general rule appears to be to leave the minimum amount possible in the paper. The difficulty will perhaps be best understood by regarding the paper-making fibres as themselves weak acids, since under normal atmospheric conditions the purest celluloses will show an acidity of pH 5 when spotted with an indicator such as, for example, methyl red. It would therefore be absurd to demand a neutral paper. If some acidity must be accepted as inevitable, with pH 5 as the lower limit and anything appreciably more acid than this as suspect, it will be evident that practical difficulties will be met in fixing definite and easily measurable limits. In practice, all the user can do is to ask a reputable paper-maker to supply paper as free as possible from excess acidity and to pay a reasonable price to justify the necessary care in manufacture.

The large-scale user of paper, however, might well use the Rasch accelerated ageing test to ensure that his papers are in fact reasonably free from acid residues and excessive alum. This test has been much used in the past for judging the permanence of paper and is still used by the United States Government in framing its specifications for archive papers. It consists in heating the sample in a water oven at 100°C for seventy-two hours in a current of air and determining the loss of resistance to folding. Although this test has many objections as an ageing test it should be admirably suited to accentuating the bad effect of excess acidity.

DAMAGE DUE TO ATMOSPHERIC POLLUTION

The commonest form of paper deterioration in temperate climates is caused by the sulphur dioxide which is present in small amounts in the atmospheres of almost all industrial countries. It is a gas smelling of burning sulphur and comes mainly from the combustion of coal and oil. The amount in general is very small —less than one volume in one million volumes of air—but in urban and industrial centres and near crowded residential areas the concentration may rise much higher. Sulphur dioxide, even at higher concentrations than is normally found in air, is not by itself harmful to paper or bookbinding materials, but when they contain small amounts of iron or copper—as is almost always the case with paper, etc., made during the last 150–200 years— these have the power to change the innocuous sulphur dioxide into the highly destructive sulphuric acid which may accumulate in paper until it reaches about 1 per cent. At this point, it will rapidly destroy the fibrous structure of paper and cause it to become brittle.

This effect was most marked about 1880–1900 when most libraries and archive stores were lighted and sometimes heated by coal gas. Coal gas contains some of the sulphur of the coal from which it was made and, when burnt in a poorly ventilated room, can give rise to relatively high concentrations of sulphur dioxide. Electricity has now largely displaced gas and open fires have given place to central heating. The damage to paper has consequently diminished in intensity but it still remains a menace to stored archives. Whilst local high concentrations of sulphur dioxide have almost disappeared, increased industrialization has resulted in moderate concentrations of sulphur dioxide becoming so widespread that it is almost impossible to avoid them.

All paper records should therefore be safeguarded against atmospheric sulphur dioxide. There are many ways of doing this but all may be classified under five heads—

1. Removal of dangerous impurities, e.g. catalytic metals, from the paper or, alternatively, preparing paper free from them.

2. Addition of alkaline or buffering substances to neutralize the sulphuric acid as it forms.

3. Sealing up the paper by coating it with an impervious varnish or by "lamination" with an impervious foil.

4. Destroying the chemical (catalytic) activity of the metallic impurities in paper by the use of inhibitors.

5. Storing paper in an atmosphere free from sulphur dioxide or other acids.

1. REMOVAL OF DANGEROUS IMPURITIES. This is scarcely an economic possibility under modern manufacturing conditions except for special uses, e.g. some photographic papers, but it is interesting, from the archivist's point of view, to note that papers made more than 200 years ago may be almost free from these impurities. It would be prudent to regard all modern paper records as vulnerable and to take the necessary steps to make them more permanent.

2. ADDITION OF ALKALINE BUFFERS. This is done as a preliminary treatment in the "Barrow" laminating process for paper by soaking the document first in a bath of lime water and then in a bath of calcium bicarbonate. These treatments add a small amount of precipitated chalk to the paper and not only remove any dangerous acids the paper may contain but provide a reserve of alkali for the future. The weakness of this process is due to the fact that slightly alkaline papers can only be immune so long as there remains some free alkali. When this is exhausted the

paper is again vulnerable. The practical value of such a method as this depends on the amount of alkali added, the amount of atmospheric pollution encountered and the exposure of the paper. Since the magnitudes of all these factors are somewhat uncertain the process will be equally uncertain.

3. SEALING THE PAPER BETWEEN IMPERVIOUS LAYERS. The best example of this is the "Barrow" lamination process. After the paper has been impregnated with chalk and dried it is heated to about 300°F as the middle layer of a sandwich composed of cellulose acetate foil $\frac{1}{1000}$ in. thick, a sheet of Jap tissue or lens tissue, the document to be protected, another sheet of Jap tissue and then another cellulose acetate foil. When sufficiently heated, the sandwich is passed through spring-loaded, heated metal rollers, rather like a domestic mangle. The sandwich emerges as a sheet slightly thicker and heavier than the original document and a good deal stiffer and stronger. The method is excellent for improving the mechanical strength of documents which are to be subjected to much handling over a period of a few years but it is too early to say how such a treated document will stand up to a polluted atmosphere, since cellulose acetate may add its quota of metallic impurities to those of the document, and is itself vulnerable to the action of sulphur dioxide in the air.

The "Sundex" process is a variant of the Barrow lamination process over which it has some advantages. It is a lamination process but uses a semi-transparent paper, glassine, in place of the cellulose acetate foil. The three components of the sandwich, the document and two sheets of glassine, are stuck together with an aqueous adhesive, such as carboxymethylcellulose (C.M.C.) or starch paste. The sandwich appears to be consolidated by pressure between heated surfaces. The process is safer than the Barrow process in that an operating temperature below that of boiling water is claimed in place of the much higher temperature of the Barrow process. In addition, the treated document has only to be soaked in water for the sandwich to fall apart yielding the original document apparently undamaged.

Its chief disadvantage, so far as can be discovered from published descriptions, is that acids are not removed from old documents as is done in the Barrow process prior to lamination. Should the document contain acid accumulated by storage in a polluted atmosphere it might be rendered more brittle by even the low temperature claimed. An important advantage is that the components of the sandwich are closely related materials and the adhesive is compatible with them both. The final sandwich is therefore much more mechanically and chemically homogeneous than a "Barrow" sandwich and consequently much less liable to unbalanced stresses due to changes in moisture content and temperature of the atmosphere.

Thus, with a few simple modifications, such as the use of inhibitors, the "Sundex" process could be made into an excellent laminating process for documents which need improvement in both mechanical durability and permanence. A variant of the Sundex process would be the use of cellophane (the non-coated kind) in place of glassine but further investigation into the permanence of this material is necessary before it can be recommended for important documents.

4. Using Inhibitors. These substances are applied to paper in much the same way as the chalk in the Barrow process, except that one bath only is needed. They can be used together with gelatine where an improvement in both chemical and mechanical properties of paper is desirable. For a description of how the impregnation is carried out, see page 37.

Some very heavily loaded papers, such as the clay surfaced art papers, contain a great deal of iron introduced with the clay, and should be given two treatments, without drying after the first treatment, and plenty of solution should be used. Buff-tinted papers, which are sometimes coloured with pigments containing iron, may be troublesome to inhibit by the process and should be given a double treatment. Usually, the buff colour changes to slightly green when the treatment has gone far enough. The great majority of writing and printing papers, however, respond readily to this treatment.

Ink marks will need to be treated cautiously. Iron-gall inks will become bluish but will not be bleached or rendered less permanent. Some of the modern inks based on soluble dyestuffs may be washed out by the inhibitor solution. Broadly speaking, inks which would normally be regarded as suitable for archive work, i.e. inks which stand a good chance of being permanent, should not suffer any diminution in permanence by treatment with the inhibitor solution, while those inks which would have been fugitive before treatment might suffer some reduction in their already poor expectation of life.

The use of inhibitors is too recent to gauge their effectiveness under practical conditions of archive storage. The process has, however, a sound theoretical and experimental basis and, unlike the alkali impregnation, remains effective so long as the inhibitor remains in the paper. Leather has been treated in a similar way for long enough to inspire confidence in its effectiveness and there seems to be no doubt that it will be equally effective for paper.

5. STORING THE DOCUMENTS IN PURIFIED AIR. In libraries and archive stores supplied with conditioned air it is usually quite easy to arrange for the conditioning plant to include an alkaline wash so that practically all acid gases are removed from the conditioned air. This is obviously the ideal method when it can be employed, since the documents need no treatment and are not only maintained free from sulphur dioxide damage but can be kept at a temperature and humidity best suited to the paper, parchment, bookbinding materials, etc., to be stored.

Many librarians prohibit smoking in the libraries under their care on the assumption that tobacco fumes are injurious to paper and books. It is very doubtful if these are likely to reach a concentration high enough to cause real damage without making the atmosphere quite intolerable to human beings, especially non-smokers. Tarry vapours and ammonia are the products sometimes cited as being the culprits. A more obvious objection to smoking is the ash which falls into the folds of the pages and soils them.

MOULDS AND FUNGI

Paper is not a very suitable medium to support the growth of moulds and fungi. However, under otherwise favourable conditions, for example tropical temperatures and high atmospheric humidity, paper will support the slow growth of these micro-organisms, some of which will have a similar action on paper to that of the dry rot fungus on wood. Not a great deal is known yet about this type of damage but it is suspected that the brown rot of paper in the tropics and the foxing of old paper in temperate climates are due to a mould which grows in the substance of the paper without giving any indication of its presence, except slight browning, until such time as the paper becomes brittle and acquires a characteristic "spicy" smell and marked brownish colour. If this suspicion is confirmed the remedies are obviously either to keep the paper dry or, if this is not possible, to incorporate a fungicide in the paper.

The question of fungicides has assumed major importance in agriculture where this kind of micro-organism finds its happy hunting ground. A similar trouble arises in the textile and paper industries due to the mildewing of cotton fabrics and paper under damp conditions of bulk storage. For these reasons, therefore, much research has been devoted to the search for even better and more effective fungicides and many of these would seem to be suitable for use for paper documents.

No single fungicide is likely to possess all the desired properties, since some of these are mutually exclusive, but from among the many substances available commercially it needs only a little discrimination to find one having a range of properties suited to almost any specific case. The following considerations are intended to be a practical guide to an interim decision in this matter.

Many fungicides are highly chlorinated organic substances and should never be used either in or near paper without the exercise of great care. These substances, while quite stable enough for most of their normal uses, may not be stable enough when they are to remain for decades or even centuries in contact with paper almost always containing impurities which accelerate the normal slow breakdown of such fungicides. An almost invariable product of this breakdown is hydrochloric acid, minute amounts of which will quickly destroy any normal paper. Therefore, before using any chlorinated organic fungicide, it is important to make sure that it is known to be reasonably stable in the presence of traces of iron, copper, manganese, etc., and that it is sufficiently effective to be of practical value when used in very small amounts, for example, of the order of 0·1 per cent of the weight of the paper.

Bearing in mind these considerations, the following substances seem suitable for use under certain conditions—

1. Salicylanilide
2. Penta-chlorphenol (P.C.P.)
3. Copper naphthenate
4. Mercuric chloride (corrosive sublimate)
5. Mercapto-benzthiazole (M.B.T.)
6. Copper oxinate, i.e. the Copper 8-hydroxy quinoline complex.

SALICYLANILIDE. One of the trade names for this substance is Shirlan, so called because it was invented by the Shirley Institute to combat mildew in cotton fabrics. From the point of view of the archivist, its properties are perhaps more desirable than those of the other four substances. (*a*) It can be applied either as an aqueous (weak alkaline) solution or as a non-aqueous solution and should be effective at a concentration of about 0·1 per cent by weight of the fabric or paper. (*b*) It has no very marked attraction for cellulose fibres and so could readily be washed out if necessary. (*c*) It is colourless and odourless and not likely to alter the appearance of paper treated with it. (*d*) It is relatively non-volatile and should render paper immune to infection from moulds for long periods at normal atmospheric temperatures. (*e*) It is *free* from chlorine.

PENTA-CHLORPHENOL (P.C.P.). This is a modern wood-preserving antiseptic and should be effective in amounts of the order of 0·1 per cent of the weight of the paper. It is highly chlorinated and must be used either in the presence of sufficient alkali to take care of any probable liberation of hydrochloric acid or in such small amounts, i.e. less than 0·1 per cent, so as not to endanger the paper even if it does decompose slightly. Like Shirlan, it can be applied as either an aqueous or non-aqueous solution, it is colourless and unlikely to give rise to an appreciable smell. It is, however, relatively volatile and this suggests its limitation in archive work—it should not be used where one treatment is expected to give lasting protection. A certain amount of judgment is called for in this connexion, however. If, for example, a large thick book is impregnated with the substance and is to be stored for long periods with only occasional use, the small volatility of P.C.P. may not be a serious matter and such a book may remain safe for centuries.

This slight volatility, on the other hand, confers one advantage on this substance; it can simplify the practical treatment of loose papers. If thin blotting paper is impregnated with, say, 1 per cent of P.C.P., it can be used for interleaving with the sheets of paper to be treated. The P.C.P. is sufficiently volatile to pass into the untreated paper after a few weeks' contact and give it some measure of protection.

COPPER NAPHTHENATE. This substance is an active fungicide and can be applied to paper as a non-aqueous solution. It is practically non-volatile and can be trusted to remain in the treated paper for periods long enough to satisfy the archivist. It should be effective at 0·1 per cent concentration and gives a slight greenish tinge to the treated paper. It is almost completely insoluble in water and is not likely to be washed out, even if the paper is immersed in water for long periods. It is suspected of causing dermatitis to susceptible skins when handled in the high concentration met with in treating fishing nets, for which it is very popular. In the low concentration needed for paper under normal storage conditions, it is not likely to cause trouble. There is a slight risk, however, that its presence in paper will increase the liability of the paper to damage in a polluted atmosphere.

MERCURIC CHLORIDE. This is one of the oldest and perhaps best known of the fungicides though it is a better antiseptic than fungicide. It is probably effective at concentrations as low as 0·1 per cent. It can be applied in aqueous or non-aqueous solution. It is colourless, odourless and non-volatile. It is somewhat liable to liberate hydrochloric acid under certain conditions but since it contains only a small proportion of chlorine and is usually effective in very low concentrations it is not very likely to be dangerous in very small amounts in practice. Its chief disadvantage is its violently poisonous nature and it should never be used except when this property is kept constantly in mind.

MERCAPTO-BENZTHIAZOLE (M.B.T.). This substance is used commercially as a rubber vulcanization accelerator. It is stated to be an effective fungicide at 0·1 per cent concentration in paper. It is free from chlorine and can be applied either as an aqueous or non-aqueous solution. A mixture of M.B.T. and Shirlan is believed to be more effective than the same amount of either substance alone. Not much is known, however, about its permanence and it does not seem to offer any material advantages over Shirlan except as regards cheapness and availability.

COPPER OXINATE. This substance has outstanding fungicidal properties and can now be obtained in forms suitable for emulsification in water or for solution in non-aqueous solvents suitable for spray-gun application. It shows promise of being effective against both mould and atmospheric damage but sufficient experimental data is not yet available to make any definite recommendations advisable.

On the whole, therefore, Shirlan is the most promising fungicide for use with paper to prevent brown rot and foxing. It may be used either as a solution in water or as a solution in carbon tetrachloride containing a small amount of acetone. The water solution is cheap and easily applied but, if large amounts of paper are to be treated, extended and properly designed drying accommodation will have to be provided. The solution in carbon tetrachloride will be more expensive and need more care in use, owing to its slightly anaesthetic property, but it can be applied by means of an ordinary lacquer spray-gun either to sheet papers or to a bound book. Under these conditions drying will be almost instantaneous but good ventilation will be necessary. The use of Shirlan has never been tried on a large scale or for long periods so that its results are still largely theoretical. However, the treatment of even valuable records by the spray-gun method seems to be quite free from risk and, until more practical data is available, it is safe to say that the risks of treatment in this way seem very much less than the ordinary risks inherent in the storage of records in warm humid climates.

ULTRA-VIOLET LIGHT

Ultra-violet light is the universal destroyer of organic matter and paper is no exception. Fortunately it is unlikely to cause the archivist much trouble chiefly because it has such poor powers of penetration. For example, most of the ultra-violet in quite strong daylight is filtered out by an ordinary glass window, even when clean. It would require a very strong source of ultra-violet to penetrate a few thicknesses of average paper and such a source is unlikely to be met with where archives are to be stored. Accidents, however, will happen and important documents could be quite adequately protected from the injurious effect of ultra-violet by storing in a cardboard container, which would be an effective barrier. If the container became brittle after long exposure it could quite cheaply be replaced. Important documents, such as The Codex Sinaiticus at the British Museum and the Declaration of Independence at Washington, are stored either in diffused light or behind a screen of amber glass. These are irreplaceable and must remain always on view to the general public and no chances can be taken. For less important documents even these precautions would seem to be excessive.

Since ultra-violet lamps are used for reading faded documents, it would be a wise precaution to make a transcript of the document the first time it is exposed to the lamp in order to avoid too frequent exposure.

BREAKDOWN DUE TO MECHANICAL AGENCIES

INSECTS. Many kinds of insect will cause damage to paper by nibbling it and boring holes through it, often not because they require the paper for food but to reach something, such as paste, which they can eat. If the paste contains an antiseptic, such as phenol, to prevent souring, it might be rather less attractive to certain insects but it certainly will not make the paper immune to attack by all insects under all conditions. Similarly, the incorporation of effective stomach poisons, unless they are also insect repellants, will not necessarily prevent insects from causing damage since they will have to attack the paper before they are killed by the poison.

Attack can therefore only be prevented by an effective repellant. A repellant substance must be relatively volatile in order to deter the insect before it attacks the paper but, being even slightly volatile, it will not remain in the paper for the long periods necessary for permanent records. Consequently, even with an effective repellant, treatment will have to be repeated at intervals.

Insect troubles must therefore be dealt with before the insect can reach the records and, in bad or difficult cases, it may be necessary to resort to methods of fumigation similar to those used by flour millers, who have to deal with infestations of a totally different order from any likely to be encountered by the archivist. The common fumigants—e.g. hydrocyanic acid, ethylene oxide/carbon dioxide, ethylene chloride/carbon tetrachloride, carbon disulphide and methyl formate/carbon dioxide—have all been shown not to be detrimental to the permanence of archive materials. They must always be applied by specialists in this field since all present some element of danger—they are either toxic to human beings, anaesthetic or inflammable. When correctly applied there is no doubt about their effectiveness.

EXCESSIVE WETNESS AND DRYNESS. Excessive dryness has often been accused of damaging paper, parchment and vellum. It is doubtful if this is strictly true, unless some other injurious condition is present at the same time. There can be no doubt that when these materials are deprived of their normal amount of moisture, by being stored in an unusually dry atmosphere, they tend to lose their suppleness and, in extreme conditions, may become brittle. If they are roughly handled in this state they may crack and be damaged mechanically.

Vellum tends to cockle with either excessive dryness or wetness but if not too badly deformed will flatten partly or completely on return to normal conditions. Excessive moisture, besides producing cockling in vellum and wrinkling in paper, has some much more serious effects. When the relative humidity of the atmosphere rises above 80 per cent (60–70 per cent is common in England while in the United States a rather wider range is experienced) parchment, vellum and paper all tend to harbour the growth of moulds and the effects can be serious (*see* p. 26). In countries with a humid climate the only two practicable methods of dealing with excessive humidity are air conditioning or the use of fungicides.

Vellum and parchment which are badly cockled can be flattened by interleaving with slightly damp paper and leaving for a few hours under slight pressure. The amount of damping is often a matter of judgment but it can be adjusted to a nicety by piling sheets of paper, for example newsprint, so that one wet sheet alternates with one or more dry sheets. If this pile is left to stand under slight pressure for a few hours to "even out" it should be possible to secure the best degree of dampness required for the interleaving with the vellum, etc. If clean unprinted newsprint is not available great care should be taken not to use ordinary newspapers, under even slight pressure, since the danger of offsetting is always present. If pressure is not used and the newspapers are evenly and only slightly damped the risk is not great but care will always be necessary.

When softening folded vellum or parchment documents which are at all likely to be hard and stiff it is best to wrap them in a slightly damp cloth for a few hours before attempting to open them out if cracked folds are to be avoided. In all cases where paper or vellum are to be damped it must be remembered that moulds can grow extremely rapidly on damp paper and still more rapidly on damp vellum and parchment and if these materials are to be kept damp for more than twenty-four hours the water for damping should contain some safe fungicide, such as thymol.

CHAPTER 4

PREVENTION OF DAMAGE TO PAPER

WHEN dealing with the books and documents which come under the care of the archivist, it is useful to keep in mind that though their actual value may be known their potential value can rarely be fully assessed. Each book or document will normally need individual consideration and the question will often arise as to the best method of finding out what treatment, if any, is to be given and how it can be given without damaging or changing them as archives.

The Public Record Office in this country sets a high standard for its own work in this respect, it makes quite sure that any repair is clearly evident, dated and, when necessary, explained. The collector of antiquities, on the other hand, frequently uses his skill to disguise any repairs he may carry out. Most archivists would agree that the attitude of the Record Office is correct where any major repair is necessary to preserve the document. But, in practice, such a clear-cut decision as this is not always possible.

GENERAL TESTING METHODS

Before treating paper with any liquid, such as a sizing bath or a fungicidal solution or merely with a damping pad, it would be wise to make sure that ink and colours will not be removed or smudged; it might be advisable to obtain some information as to the mechanical strength of the paper, its acidity or even its fibre and mineral composition.

By using refined techniques and some manipulative skill, the information needed can often be obtained from some small and unimportant part of the document, such as the extreme corner of a flyleaf or even the flourish of a signature, using only an area of paper of one square millimetre. Such manipulations can give valuable information and are practically invisible and harmless. Only a purist would insist on recording each of such operations. It is therefore well worth while to acquire some skill in these fine "micro" tests.

To determine the composition of paper the specialist will use a fine bent needle to scrape a few fibres from some inconspicuous margin or corner of the paper, will transfer this to a microscope slide and, by using methods well known to the paper chemist, he can usually give a good and fairly quantitative analysis of the fibre furnish of the sample. Often, he can also give some idea of the kind of treatment the fibres have had at the hands of the manufacturer.

However, the archivist himself can carry out some of the simpler tests which may serve as a useful guide when deciding how to treat any book or document. He will need some small chemist's pipettes, such as those commonly in use for determining acidities by the indicator method and for "spot" tests. These consist of 3 in. lengths of capillary glass tube with a small india-rubber bulb at one end. These are quite simple to handle after a little practice. With them minute drops of liquids can be applied to paper without undue spreading. Using one of these pipettes, or even a simple piece of glass tube drawn out to a fine point, a tiny drop of water can be applied to paper to indicate the state of the sizing. On well-sized paper the droplet will remain on the surface for some minutes.

If the paper of a book has been appreciably damaged by atmospheric sulphur dioxide a drop of water applied to the centre and another at the edge of the page will usually show quite clearly whether the edge has been damaged. If it has been damaged the size will have broken down and the paper will absorb the water like blotting paper. Similarly, if one drop of water is applied to the centre of a foxmark and another outside the mark, the difference between their rates of absorption will show the severity of the foxing. The paper under an old fox-mark will often be as brittle and porous as acid damaged paper.

Again, small spots of indicators can be used to find out the acidity of paper. Two useful indicators for determining acidity are methyl orange and congo red. If the proper "reagent quality" dyes are bought they will often be in bottles labelled with the colour changes corresponding to different pH values. In this connexion, pH 5 is the acidity given by pure cellulose. Alkalinity is usually not so important to determine as excess acidity. The above indicators will not serve to determine any pH value higher than about 5.

Samples of inks and colours can be removed for analysis by placing one or more minute drops of water or other reagent where they can do no harm, leaving for a few minutes and then absorbing them on pieces of special filter paper which can then be used for analysis. This, however, is work for the specialist but the archivist should know roughly what can be done in case of need.

In these and other ways, much valuable information can often be gained without damage to the paper. The light fastness of inks and colours can be tested by screening all but a minute area of paper which can then be exposed to the light of an ultra-violet lamp and the fading of the ink or colour observed under a hand lens.

This kind of technique has been brought to perfection by the specialists who examine art treasures, and laboratories for its application exist in connexion with the British Museum and the National Gallery. There is one warning about making judgments from these "micro" tests: the part tested may not be representative of the whole. Where any such doubt exists it will be necessary to test a number of suitably spaced spots and decide from the results what reliance is to be placed on their indications.

A surprising amount of information about the composition of paper and inks can be obtained by a skilful use of the ultra-violet lamp without in any way damaging either the document or the ink. An excellent description of this kind of work is given by Grant in *Books and Documents*, a copy of which should be on every archivist's work bench.

TREATMENT OF PAPER AND BOUND BOOKS
WITH FUNGICIDE (SHIRLAN)

A general discussion of the causes which lead to the need for treating paper with fungicides will be found on page 26. The following details are given to assist in the practical application of these agents. Two forms of the treatment are given, one making use of an aqueous solution and unsuited to the treatment of bound books, the other using a non-aqueous solution and suitable for loose papers and, with some limitations, for bound books.

Neither should be used for vellum. The non-aqueous solution may tend to dissolve certain of the plastics sometimes used for covering the boards of a book. As a safeguard, a little of the solution should be rubbed with the tip of the finger on an inconspicuous part of the plastic covering or on any other part about which there may be some doubt. If the solution is likely to cause damage the part being rubbed will feel sticky. In this case, the plastic covering should be removed if the non-aqueous treatment is to be given.

Aqueous Solution of Shirlan

Water soluble Shirlan	. .	$\frac{1}{2}$ oz
Water .	. . .	$1\frac{1}{2}$ gallons

Dissolve the Shirlan in a small amount of warm water and add to the bulk of cold water. The solution will be ready for use when it is clear.

The treatment is simple enough to be carried out without special apparatus or skill and is applicable to almost any kind of paper, board or linen with, however, a few limitations in practice. In the first place, it may be unsuitable for papers which are so badly embrittled that they would be too weak to handle in the wet state. In the second place, since modern inks are extremely diverse in character, it would be unwise to wet any document having ink writing on it without making some of the tests mentioned on page 34.

The impregnation is quite straightforward. The paper is allowed to soak in the cold or slightly warmed solution for a few minutes, removed from the solution when soaked through, blotted or squeezed to remove surplus liquid and hung up to dry in air at room temperature. When almost dry, the paper can be pressed to flatten it and the drying completed. The impregnation, though simple to carry out, can be very messy unless carried out systematically, and the following directions indicate one way which is simple and tidy, requiring only a large photographic developing dish and some suitable arrangements for drying.

As most papers absorb up to twice their weight of solution, sufficient solution should be prepared to supply twice the weight of paper to be impregnated, plus enough to leave about 1 in. deep in the developing dish, which should if possible be large enough to take the largest piece of paper to be treated when fully opened out. Enough solution is then poured into the dish to give a bath 1–2 in. deep and the sheets of paper are added one at a time, making sure that each is submerged before the next one is added.

A pile of sheets can be built up in the dish until there is barely enough liquid to cover the last sheet. The wet pile is then lifted out of the dish, turned over on to a sheet of glass and *gently* squeegeed with a roller-type squeegee until excess solution has been squeezed out of the pile. The sheets can then be lifted off one at a time and hung up to dry.

While the pile of paper is being built up in the impregnating bath, the bottom sheet will generally have had time to become thoroughly impregnated and, by turning the pile over before squeegeeing, the well-impregnated bottom sheet will be taken off first. Before reaching the last sheet this will have had a chance to soak thoroughly.

The rate of soaking of paper can be materially hastened by using the bath warm or by adding one part in one thousand (a few drops to a pint) of a spreading agent. There are so many spreading agents that some caution is necessary in order to make sure that a safe one is chosen. Perhaps the safest agents are those of the so-called "non-ionic" type. One example of this type is the common washing liquid called "Stergene."

Since papers vary enormously in composition and since some old papers contain harmful and coloured decomposition products, it is usually advisable to keep one bath for each kind of paper to be treated. If this is not possible, a large volume of solution should be used, i.e. a deep bath for a small amount of paper, so that any harmful products extracted from one paper will be too much diluted to spoil another. Some old papers contain enough acid to spoil the bath; they increase its acidity until the active constituent, Shirlan, is thrown out of solution. If the solution looks at all cloudy it should be rejected and fresh solution used.

The aqueous impregnating solution is unsuitable for use by large libraries, where the drying of large amounts of wet paper would be troublesome, and in cases where books, written manuscripts and colour plates would have to be treated. The following solution and treatment are suitable for a wider range of archives and could be used much more conveniently.

A stock of mixed solvent is made as follows—

Stabilized trichlorethylene . .	19 parts by volume
Acetone	1 part by volume

The "Shirlan" solution is made from—

Mixed solvent . . .	5 pints
Shirlan	1 oz

This should be sprayed on to the document from one of the conventional lacquer spray-guns. The operation should always be carried out under conditions of very good ventilation since trichlorethylene, though non-inflammable, is slightly anæsthetic, and the spray should not be breathed.

With practice, most of the spray should be received by the paper to be treated, which needs spraying on one side only.

The amount required—about 10 per cent of the weight of the paper—should evaporate within a few seconds of application, so that the paper should not require a special drying operation before storage. With care, books can be sprayed page by page without rebinding, but exceptional bindings—those not using conventional materials, e.g. leather, linen and buckram—might need special care and protection in case the material would be injured by the solvent. In general, the use of the spray technique will call for adequate subsidiary equipment and should not be undertaken on a large scale without it.

This equipment consists of a spray-gun and air compressor working at 30–50 lb per square inch with an adequately ventilated spray booth. It is unlikely to be available to any but the very large libraries and archive stores. It is, however, often available in garages and car repair shops and, provided adequate precautions are taken, this equipment could be made to serve the archivists' needs. It would be much more satisfactory, however, to institute central stations where the equipment and skilled operation would be available to all at a reasonable price.

A third possibility would be to dilute the foregoing solution to ten times the strength given, i.e. $\frac{1}{10}$ oz to five pints of mixed solvent. If this is used as recommended for the aqueous bath the impregnated sheets will dry very rapidly without any provision for extensive drying racks. It should be remembered, when using this solution, that the rubber of the squeegee may be attacked by it; so also might a plastic dish. The dish should, therefore, be of earthenware or enamelled iron and, instead of squeegeeing the pile of wet papers, it would be preferable either to squeeze it by pressing with the flat of the hand or with a piece of clean wood or, alternatively, to allow it to drain a while.

TREATMENT OF PAPER WITH INHIBITORS

These agents can at present only be applied in aqueous solution. It is hoped that, as a result of work now being carried out, it may become possible to carry out the impregnation with non-aqueous solutions and so make feasible the treatment of bound volumes, without rebinding, in the manner described for the non-aqueous impregnation with fungicide.

The aqueous solution is made up as follows—

Disodium pyrophosphate	.	. $1\frac{1}{2}$ oz
Potassium ferrocyanide .	.	. $\frac{1}{6}$ oz
(Yellow prussiate)		
Soda crystals (washing soda)	.	. $\frac{1}{2}$ oz
Water		. 1 gallon

The washing soda is not essential to the efficacy of the solution but is added to prevent the paper turning greenish after treatment. If a slight tint is not objectionable the soda free solution will colour the paper after treatment, a slight greenish colour where there is iron, and a pinkish colour where there is copper. These colours indicate clearly that the paper has been treated. The ferrocyanide will not dissolve very quickly unless it is in powder form. When all the solids are dissolved the solution will be ready for use. The impregnation is carried out as described for the aqueous solution of Shirlan (*see* p. 37).

The inhibitor solution may be made up with an addition of glue or gelatine if the paper to be treated is to be sized. Gelatine is preferable if the final colour of the paper is important but the bath will need to be kept warm to prevent gelatinization. If, however, a slight yellowing is not objectionable a good quality of pale cabinet maker's glue should be used. The solution can then be used at room temperature without setting. For the sizing of normal papers, 3 oz of glue or gelatine, well softened in water and dissolved by gentle warming, should be added to the above solution.

The speed of soaking with these solutions can be increased by warming or by the addition of spreading agents as described for the Shirlan solution. The same precautions will also be necessary in the treatment of acid or discoloured papers.

The acidity of the bath can be controlled by placing a drop of it on a strip of neutral litmus paper. The freshly made-up bath will leave the litmus a purplish colour; if it is too acid the colour will change to red. The bath could be corrected by adding more soda until the litmus is again purple, but it is usually preferable to discard the bath since it will most likely be sufficiently coloured to spoil white paper.

CHAPTER 5

PARCHMENT AND VELLUM

THE question of the permanence of parchment or vellum scarcely ever arises. These materials have lasted for many centuries and, since modern manufacturing methods are in essence the same as they have been in the past, there is no reason to suppose that the present-day materials will not have an equally long life.

Animal skins first came into use when the imported Egyptian papyrus became too expensive and difficult to obtain. There can be little to choose between the two materials as regards permanence but no doubt the early users soon learned to appreciate the superior strength of vellum and also found out how to combat its susceptibility to damp. It is interesting to note that the early writers on vellum probably used the same carbon inks as were used for papyrus and discovered that these could readily be washed off, leaving little trace behind. It is supposed that iron-gall inks were devised to overcome this disadvantage. Even these can be removed by washing and scrubbing, though not so completely as the carbon inks, hence the palimpsests with their ghostly reminders of a previous text.

MANUFACTURING PROCESSES

The manufacture of vellum, as carried out at present near London, is essentially a skilled craft, using very little machinery and relying largely on manual dexterity. The salt pickled skins—sheep, goat, calf and sometimes pig—are first washed in running water to remove dirt, blood, etc., and then allowed to soak for a few days in lime and water in pits in order to loosen the hair and soften the skins. Simple machinery scrapes off the hair and removes some of the flesh. The cleaned skins are put back into lime pits for some weeks and then re-fleshed and washed.

The calf, goat or pig skins intended for vellum are stretched while wet on wooden frames and washed with hot water. After being scraped with blunt "half-moon" shaped knives, to remove as much fat as possible, they are coated with whiting and allowed to dry thoroughly. When quite dry the skins are shaved to the correct thickness with sharp "half-moon" scrapers.

Sheepskins to be used for making parchment are, before stretching, split into skivers (grain side) and flesh. The skivers go for tanning, while the best of the flesh splits are stretched on frames, as for vellum, swilled with hot water and scraped with blunt knives to remove as much fat as possible. They are then covered with whiting, allowed to dry and scraped to the required thickness. After this, the skins are again washed, scraped with a blunt knife and dried.

This bare outline scarcely hints at the skill required to produce good vellum and parchment, skill which might have been almost a lost art today had it not been for the popularity of percussion instruments in modern dance bands.

PERMANENCE AND DURABILITY

Very little needs to be said about the treatment of vellum to take advantage of its natural permanence and durability. These qualities are no doubt largely due to the imperviousness of the skin. Impurities which might be introduced during manufacture remain on the surface from which they can readily be removed by scraping. The high alkalinity of all the solutions used in the processing ensures that dangerous metals are maintained in a highly insoluble condition throughout the manufacture. The treatment of the skin in lime, a proportion of which remains in the substance of the skin throughout its preparation, ensures that a reserve of basic substance is present in the finished material to neutralize any acids which may gain entrance from polluted atmospheres. The great mechanical strength of both parchment and vellum gives them lasting resistance to mechanical stresses and attritional wear.

TREATMENT OF VELLUM AND PARCHMENT
FOR ARCHIVES

It has been stated that vellum must not be kept too dry or it will become brittle. It would perhaps be more correct to say that it becomes hornier and would probably return to its natural suppleness when returned to a normal atmosphere. In a horny condition it could possibly be damaged by excessive bending and creasing which is hardly the normal treatment for the pages of a book though it may be for large documents (*see* p. 31).

Dampness is the real enemy of these materials, causing them to cockle and ultimately to rot. Owing to a high degree of imperviousness, especially of vellum, it would be difficult to impregnate them effectively with a fungicide and, in practice, they must be kept dry if they are to last. A relative humidity of 60–75 per cent should be suitable at temperatures of 40–70°F.

It is almost impossible to treat parchment and vellum to render them unfit for insects to eat, so the only remedy here is to prevent the access of insects.

CHAPTER 6

INKS

THE earliest inks were essentially suspensions of carbon (soot) in gum. They were quite suitable for use with papyrus which would be porous enough to absorb the ink and entrap the pigment (soot) between the fibres. Under these conditions the writing would be both permanent and indelible and harmless to the papyrus. Ainsworth Mitchell states that this type of ink was in common use until the eleventh century when iron-gall inks began to come into prominence.

He suggests that the use of parchment and vellum made iron-gall inks essential since carbon-gum inks would not adhere to greasy vellum and in any case could be readily removed by sponging. It is interesting to note, in this connexion, that the Lindisfarne gospels—supposed to date from the seventh century— are written on vellum with iron-gall ink which is still black and clearly legible after more than a thousand years. Blagden's report on his examination of vellum MSS. of the ninth to the fifteenth centuries shows that all were written in iron-gall ink in which no trace of pigment (carbon) could be found.

Nevertheless, carbon-containing inks continued to be used for documents, probably until the advent of the "blue-black" ink period. It is quite probable that small amounts of carbon pigment were used to make the iron-gall inks more legible immediately after writing.

From these somewhat indefinite beginnings, simple iron-gall inks held the field until about 1860 when the invention of aniline dyes brought about radical changes in ink manufacture for, with their use, the need for partial oxidation of iron-gall inks no longer existed. Since this time ink manufacture has become extremely complicated.

COMPOSITION OF MODERN INKS

The old, simple iron-gall inks were made by mixing ferrous sulphate (copperas) with an infusion of oak galls or other tannin containing vegetable matter. Before exposure to air this liquid is almost colourless and thinly fluid. If used on paper or vellum the writing is at first barely visible; it sinks rapidly into paper with a tendency to spread (feathering). After a few days, the writing becomes a dense black due to the oxidation of the soluble, almost colourless ferrous tannate of the fresh ink to the deep black, insoluble ferric tannate which is permanent and, in the case of paper, is fixed in the fibre. The oxidation is brought about by oxygen from the air. The feathering can be reduced by adding gum or similar thickening agent to the ink or, alternatively, by sizing the paper. If the ink in the inkwell comes into contact with the air, oxidation sets in and the ink darkens and eventually becomes muddy due to formation of the insoluble ferric tannate. The original inks were allowed to undergo a controlled oxidation before use in order to give the writing sufficient immediate blackness to enable the writer to see what he was doing. If, at this stage, a small amount of a strong acid, usually hydrochloric or sulphuric, is added to the ink, further oxidation, with its associated muddiness, is very much delayed. This modification would also delay the blackening of the writing on the paper but this would not now matter as the writing would be legible from the start. The writing with these inks may require some weeks to develop its full blackness on paper.

By the addition of an aniline dye, the almost colourless freshly-made ink could be given sufficient immediate colour to avoid the necessity for a preliminary oxidation, while sufficient acid could be added to slow down the oxidation of the ink to such an extent that it did not quickly become muddy in the inkwell. This iron-gall-dye mixture became the popular Stephens blue-black ink. It was easy to write with on sized paper, it became deep black with age and was permanent enough for important archive work but it was rather too acid for steel pens and on the danger line for paper.

It is easy to appreciate the dilemma of the manufacturer of the period. He naturally wanted to add enough acid to give his ink a long life in the inkwell but was restrained by the fear that he would be shortening the life of the pens and the paper. That he overdid the acid in many instances is evident from old paper documents which have sometimes been perforated by the writing while remaining quite sound elsewhere.

Most modern inks are made to overcome one or more of the disadvantages inherent in blue-black inks—their acidity, muddiness and not-quite-perfect permanence. The impermanence, incidentally, is rather different from that of the aniline dye inks. If exposed too much to light, the ferric tannate pigment of the ink may be oxidized by the air until, finally, the tannic acid part of it is destroyed leaving the brown mineral ferric oxide behind. This appears as a brown ghost of the original writing and can be made visible by ultra-violet light, or by development with tannic acid solution to re-form ferric tannate or with potassium ferrocyanide solution to form Prussian blue. The so-called impermanence of iron-gall inks is thereby only partial. If the fading writing is re-developed to Prussian blue it would probably be more permanent that the original, at any rate as regards fastness to light.

MODERN WRITING INKS FOR PAPER

Although iron-gall inks are still extensively used for records where permanence is important they have been almost entirely superseded for use with modern fountain and ball-point pens. Since the early days of the synthetic dye industry the first brilliant but fugitive dyes have been greatly improved in variety and fastness, often without much sacrifice of tinctorial power. It is natural that solutions of these should be used as inks since they can be made free from acid and without any tendency to become muddy.

Nevertheless, before describing these modern modifications, it is worth mentioning that a special, so-called record ink is still made and sold in England. It is a straight iron-gall ink containing a satisfactory amount of iron and gall extract and is free from any added dyestuff or colouring matter. In use it starts by being pale but visible, while in about twenty-four hours the writing becomes jet black, insoluble in water and light fast. This ink will be mentioned again when dealing with inks for vellum.

The dyes used for ink manufacture are so numerous that it would be impracticable to do more than give a general summary of their properties as these affect the permanence of paper documents written with them. The two commonest defects of these inks are poor light fastness and solubility in water or other solvent. Certain substantive dyes have been used which, on drying, become fixed on the fibre. These inks are sometimes rather strongly alkaline (pH 12–13) and very fast to light.

For the most part, however, the dyes most commonly used remain soluble in water or alcohol on drying. A small drop of water or alcohol on an inconspicuous part of the writing will readily show up any spreading due to solubility. The chief objection to soluble ink is that if the document accidentally becomes wet or even damp the writing may become illegible due to spreading or smearing. A further objection is that, if a simple solvent or washing treatment removes the ink without leaving a trace, the way is open to falsification and the Courts may refuse to accept as evidence a document written in such ink.

Light fastness varies from a few hours in bright sunshine, in the case of the brilliant basic mauves, blues, greens and magentas, to the near permanence of the vat dyes. Normally, moderate fastness is good enough for all but specially important archives. Iron-gall inks work so badly with fountain pens that it is hardly surprising that they have been replaced by "dye" inks for this purpose.

Ball-Point Inks

The situation regarding the newer ball-point inks is similar. The ball-point mechanism will work badly with an iron-gall ink, not only on account of the muddiness which may develop with this kind of ink, but also because of its acidity. The composition of inks used by the makers of these pens, which is usually a closely guarded secret, consists, in most cases, of solutions of fairly light fast dyes in an oily solvent. They have two outstanding disadvantages as regards permanence—they are readily soluble in alcohol and other non-aqueous solvents and they do not sink deeply into the paper. They can therefore easily be removed, either by soaking in spirit or by removing the extreme top surface of the paper with a rubber eraser.

A more recent modification of the ball-point inks is used in the so-called "liquid lead" pencil which is like a ball-point pen but filled with a pasty emulsion containing very finely divided graphite. It makes a mark, resembling that from a lead pencil, which, it is claimed, can readily be removed by a rubber eraser. A simple test of one of these "pencil" marks on a hard writing paper suggests that the mark is only removed by removing at the same time the surface of the paper and the rather gritty nature of the rubber supplied by the makers tends to confirm this.

On the other hand, the "pencil" mark resists solvents very well, better, in fact, than the ball-point ink mark. This suggests that the inclusion of a pigment, such as lamp black, in ball-point ink might enable it to give writing which would be not only light fast but solvent proof and so good enough for most archive work. The fact that the ball-point gives a very superficial writing which could be readily removed by a rubber eraser is perhaps not so important since damage to the surface of paper can usually be easily detected.

Two methods have been suggested for increasing the fastness of ball-point inks. The dyes used for these inks are frequently basic dyes which have usually poor light and solvent fastness; they will, however, combine with phospho-tungstic and phospho-molybdic acids to give insoluble lakes with fairly good light fastness and excellent solvent fastness. If, therefore, paper is impregnated with one of these substances the usual ball-point ink will make a reasonably permanent mark on it. Alternatively, the impregnation can be carried out after the writing has been done. If a substance such as pyrogallol is included in the composition of the ink, the dyes used can be made much more light fast although their solvent fastness will not be appreciably improved.

An interesting attempt to avoid the chief disadvantages of iron-gall inks, namely acidity and muddiness, resulted in an ink which was in effect a colloidal solution of Prussian blue. It gave writing which was extremely fast to light, water and the hypochlorite (bleach) solutions often used as liquid ink erasers. It was, however, bleached by alkalis, it attacked the 14-carat gold nibs of fountain pens and it could not be mixed with other inks.

INKS FOR VELLUM AND PARCHMENT

Modern vellum or parchment documents have usually been sufficiently important to escape the fountain and ball-point pens. They are usually written in iron-gall ink or in one of the carbon-gum inks. The carbon-gum inks are used surprisingly often, probably with the idea of matching the known permanence of the two materials. It should be remembered, however, that such an ink is carried on the extreme surface only and could be removed by sponging or other simple means.

An iron-gall ink, on the other hand, bites into the surface of both vellum and parchment and may even penetrate some distance into the more porous parchment so that it will be much more difficult to remove. Even the attrition caused by the frequent sliding of sheets of vellum over one another may have some effect on the carbon-gum but much less on the iron-gall writing. The latter is also freer from the sometimes unwelcome shine of permanent (waterproof) indian inks. The early manuscript writers knew these facts which are quite often forgotten or ignored by present-day writers.

In order to overcome the natural greasiness of parchment and vellum and to enable them to take the ink better, it is usual to roughen their surfaces by pouncing with finely-powdered pumice. This may tend to spoil the attractive grain of natural goat vellum used for binding. Pouncing can be rendered much less necessary by adding about one part of a spreading agent to one thousand parts of record ink. Ink modified in this way should not be used on paper without a preliminary test, since it may cause feathering unless the paper is well sized. In any case, even for vellum, a larger amount of spreading agent should not be used.

TYPEWRITER INKS

It seems likely that typewritten documents will figure increasingly in the archivist's outlook and may, one day, outnumber the printed and written documents. The handy, versatile, mechanical scribe known as a typewriter was frowned upon by the solicitor and civil servant in the early days of its development, probably largely on the ground of the facilities it seemed to offer to the forger and falsifier. There can be few today who would object to its use, even for important documents. Apart from the mechanical uniformity of the type faces, which might facilitate unauthorized substitution, there is the question of the permanence of the typewriter inks, their fastness to light, erasure and solvents.

It will be convenient for the present purpose to classify these inks in three categories—

1. Typewriter ribbon and stamp-pad inks
2. Carbon tissues ⎫ Typewriter copying processes
3. Duplicator inks ⎭

Stamp pads are included with typewriter ribbons because the same kinds of inks are used for both.

Typewriter Ribbon and Stamp-Pad Inks

It is now almost universal practice to use ink-impregnated ribbons for modern typewriters and these ribbons appear to conform fairly closely to a general pattern. The modern ribbon is made from a thin, tough textile fabric impregnated with an oily base carrying oil-soluble dyes or insoluble pigments. The black pigment is usually some form of carbon and, for this reason, black ribbons and black stamp pads can almost always be relied upon for permanence.

It might be supposed that the impression from a typewriter ribbon or stamp would be very superficial on paper but the fact that the medium is a liquid oil accounts for quite a considerable amount of slow penetration of the ink into the paper until, after a day or two, it will have sunk sufficiently deep to become much more proof against erasure. The same slow movement of the ink in the ribbon ensures that it will be more uniformly exhausted by continued use than would have been the case had the ink been pasty or solid.

Coloured ribbons, such as the common purple one, often contain fugitive dyes and sometimes also a small amount of carbon pigment to give greater opacity to the colour of the impression. These pigmented inks share to some extent the fastness of the black inks, not only to light but also to solvents. There is a tendency to make the modern coloured ribbon and stamp-pad inks with the "light fast" phosphotungstate or phosphomolybdate lakes and these should be permanent enough for most archive purposes.

It is a curious fact that if a typed document written with an ink containing a pigment such as lampblack is steeped in a solvent for the vehicle, the pigment tends to sink deeper into the fibres of the paper instead of being washed off. The writing may be smudged but it should be much more difficult to erase mechanically than before. This effect is most surprising with carbon copies.

Typewriter Copying Processes

The copying processes most commonly used in connexion with the typewriter can be classified as—

1. Hecktographs
2. Carbon tissues
3. Stencils
4. Offset litho

1. HECKTOGRAPHS. These processes make use mainly of soluble "dye" inks. The special ribbons for this kind of work are impregnated with glycerine or similar "humectant" carrying a water-soluble dye. The typed document is pressed against a moist gelatine or clay surface until some of the dye from the ink diffuses into the moist surface. If clean sheets of paper are pressed

into contact with these surfaces they can be made to take an impression which resembles the original typed document. A modification of this process uses a special carbon tissue containing a spirit-soluble dye which is used to give a "master" copy on the back of a sheet of paper. This is then pressed in contact with clean sheets of paper damped with a non-aqueous solvent for the dye.

In all these processes the ink must be soluble, either in water or in the special solvent used, and this inherent inability to take advantage of the fastness of insoluble pigments constitutes the fundamental disadvantage of the hecktograph processes from the point of view of permanence. Incidentally, hecktograph copies can usually be distinguished by their diffused outline. This kind of copy is not suitable for archive work though, if necessary, its permanence can often be improved by bathing the document in a weak solution of phosphotungstic or phosphomolybdic acid in order to mordant the dye.

2. CARBON TISSUES. Where only a few copies are required, the carbon tissue is commonly used. The "blackness" rule applies to this method and the ink in this case consists of a solid wax vehicle containing carbon (lampblack) or wax soluble dyes coated on thin strong paper.

The "carbon" impression left by the typewriter key cannot sink into the paper, as happens with the fluid ribbon inks, and it tends to remain entirely on the surface where it can be erased fairly easily with a pencil eraser. If a carbon copy is treated with a solvent for wax the pigment, if any, tends to sink deeper into the paper and, though it may be badly smudged, the copy is usually quite legible.

Should carbons be used for archive work? If they are black they will usually be fast to light and solvent but not necessarily fast to erasure and, with the hard-surfaced papers sometimes used for these copies, erasure may be difficult to trace. Apart from this fault, carbons should be fairly permanent if black and it would not be difficult to make coloured tissues using the more permanent lakes.

3. STENCILS. This is a common duplicating method where more than a hundred copies of a typewritten document are required. The typing is done on a sheet of fabric covered with wax or cellulose, which becomes porous to ink where it is struck by the type. This master sheet is then used to cover a clean sheet of paper while ink is forced through the porous parts of the master with a squeegee or similar device. Stencil inks follow the "blackness" rule. They lend themselves to the use of pigments and there is no reason, apart from cost, for using fugitive colours.

The paper used for taking the copies has to be fairly porous in order to absorb the ink quickly to prevent offsetting. The porosity of the paper ensures that the ink will sink well into the fibres and therefore will be difficult to erase without leaving visible evidence. There is no reason why black stencil copies should not be at least as permanent as the paper used for them. Stencil inks may have either an oil or a glycerine vehicle; modern inks are more likely to have an oil base.

4. OFFSET LITHO. This method is adapted for office use from the offset litho printing process and is used where a large number of copies of a typewritten document are required. The record is typed on a thin, prepared metal (zinc) sheet, using a greasy ink. If its surface is kept moist the writing will pick up greasy ink from an inked roller while the rest of the surface will reject it. If a clean sheet of paper is now pressed against this inked metal sheet it will take an impression of the writing. The inks for this process are all necessarily oil based and there is no reason why fast pigments should not be used. Here, again, blackness almost always means permanence and even colours could also be permanent.

GENERAL REMARKS ON THE PERMANENCE OF TYPEWRITER INKS

If these inks are black they are very likely, with the exception of hecktograph inks which do not follow the "blackness" rule, to be permanent, fast to light, erasure and to solvents. Black carbon copies are not quite eraser proof; the other inks could not easily be erased without leaving a trace of damage to the surface of the paper. Except for hecktograph copies, modern processes should be able to make use of fairly permanent coloured inks and, in case of need, the impression from a "dye" ink can often be made much more permanent by treating the paper with a mordant, e.g. phosphomolybdic acid. In general terms, therefore, typewriter inks are much more likely to be permanent than had hitherto been thought possible.

PRINTING INKS

There is rarely any reason to doubt the permanence of printing inks. The "blackness" rule—that lampblack (soot) is not only the cheapest of pigments but also the most permanent—applies to them with full force, since they are usually black and are almost always based on pigment suspensions in a varnish base. The archivist, therefore, need concern himself only with a few of the modern modifications of quick-drying blacks and with the whole range of coloured inks, especially those used for colour reproduction.

One of the worries besetting the printer is due to offsetting, that is to undried ink from one printed sheet marking the back of the sheet following it. Many devices have been tried to overcome this nuisance, most of which are not of much interest as regards permanence. Two, however, have some bearing on permanence. One device consists in suspending the pigment in a waxy medium; this is printed on the paper in a molten condition and solidifies almost immediately. Another device is to make up the ink with a volatile solvent which evaporates sufficiently quickly to give a rapid initial drying. It is probable that the blackness rule applies to these cases also, but there might be a slight risk that some unexpected composition has been tried. The application of minute drops of water, alcohol or other solvent to some obscure part of the sheet will give some idea of the fastness of the ink to solvents (*see* p. 34). If the ink shows no smudging it may be taken as being safe enough for all normal requirements. Specially valuable documents should always be left to the specialist for examination.

With coloured inks, poor light fastness is likely to be the chief trouble. It can always be roughly assessed by exposing a small area to an intense light—ultra-violet or daylight—for a few hours. Modern coloured inks are being increasingly made from lake pigments with a base of phosphotungstic or phosphomolybdic acid and these are outstandingly fast by comparison with the old alum lakes. Nevertheless, when an exceptionally transparent colour is required, the printer may use one of the older lakes.

Illustrations are frequently reproduced on coated art papers and these may shed their coatings with wear or under damp conditions. The illustration will probably disappear with the coating and there is little that one can do about this except to spray the whole sheet with some fixative as used by artists. The more commonly occurring cellulose lacquers and fixatives with a base of nitro-cellulose should not be used if permanence is essential. These coated art papers are not inherently less stable than ordinary printing papers but they are mechanically weak and troublesome, especially to the bookbinder, on account of this tendency to delaminate, and fixative must only be used sparingly in order not to accentuate it.

CHAPTER 7

SEWING MATERIALS

LINEN and silk fabrics have survived from pre-Christian eras and samples can be seen in our museums. While it is true that many of these museum specimens are only held together by special treatment, it is equally true to say that both materials are known to last from 500 to 1,000 years without losing more than a small part of their strength. It is, therefore, reasonable to suppose that well-made threads composed of these materials will be satisfactory for durable bindings.

THREADS

Good linen thread is reasonably cheap while silk is not too expensive for high-class work and it would be difficult, apart from cost, to decide in favour of either. Good cotton thread would, possibly, be acceptable but, since linen thread is reasonably cheap, stronger than cotton, and known to be satisfactory after centuries of practical use, it should be quite unnecessary to use cotton. Ramie and the different hemps, e.g. sisal and manilla, have much in common with linen but as they are not in general use there is no point in using them if linen and silk are available.

The newer synthetic fibres call for serious consideration by the bookbinder because of their very attractive qualities. They are extremely strong, surpassing even silk in this respect, and the individual filaments in the thread are continuous and uniform. They are unique in that each filament has been stretched to about four times its length after spinning so that every inch of every filament may be said to have been given a rigorous testing before it is assembled in the form of thread.

Accelerated ageing tests, which are considered by many to be much too drastic for paper and textiles, have very little effect on

"Nylon 66" and "Terylene." These synthetics are free from any tendency to rot when damp and they retain a large part of their dry strength on wetting. They are also almost free from contaminating metals which might tend to cause impermanence in polluted atmospheres. All these advantages call for serious thought and it is the writer's belief that the new materials will ultimately displace the traditional threads.

One disadvantage of using silk, nylon or Terylene thread is their liability to unravel and "catch up" during sewing. This can be avoided by soaking the thread in polyvinyl acetate emulsion, diluted to about three times its original volume with water, and drying it in the air. This treatment slightly glues together the individual filaments of the thread which is then as convenient to use as ordinary linen thread. It also ensures that the tension is shared equally among all the filaments and not thrown on to one only, as might otherwise occur if one filament in a loose bundle was slightly tighter than the rest. The effect of P.V.A. is therefore similar to that of the tar in tarred rope: it prevents fraying and unequal stressing of the individual strands. The use of P.V.A. with silk, nylon and Terylene does not appear to have any adverse effect when the accelerated ageing test is applied, though it naturally reduces their softness and flexibility somewhat.

CORDS AND TAPES

Many of the arguments in favour of linen, hemp, silk and the synthetics apply also to materials for cords and tapes. For tape for the library type of binding (French joint), strips of vellum are much superior to the usual textile tape and the known durability of vellum, together with its toughness, make it an almost ideal material for this purpose. Its great disability, however, is its high water absorption and consequent liability to rot in damp situations. If nylon or Terylene braid or ribbon can be obtained they might well be superior to vellum.

For cords and thongs for very large books, tawed pigskin, multiple vellum strips or catgut suggest themselves, as being durable and strong enough for good-class work. Sisal hemp fibre, while too coarse and harsh to be used as a sewing material, is worth consideration as a material for the cords of very large and even medium-sized books. This fibre is extremely strong and durable in the form of binder twine. It is the only cheap fibre strong enough to stand the gruelling treatment given by a combine harvester or self-binder, and it is used for the cordage of yachts, though it is not as popular as manilla hemp. It would seem worth while to use it for medium-heavy to heavy work where its coarseness and stiffness are no disadvantage. If ordinary binder twine is cut into 12 in. lengths, knotted at one end and well teased out to remove loose fibres, knotted at the other end and, with the first knot united, teased out and freed from the remaining short fibres, it will usually yield about 50–70 per cent of its weight of parallel full-length fibres. These refined fibres are excellent for the raised cords in full flexible binding—they are sufficiently flexible, they allow the sections to be slid over them during rounding and backing and they give slips as strong as the cords themselves. This strength of the slips is available at the joints where it is most needed and where it is usually lacking owing to the demands of neatness.

FACTORS AFFECTING DURABILITY AND PERMANENCE

By whatever standard method a book is bound—flexible, library or "sawn in"—its life depends more completely on the thread, cords or tapes than on any other structural component, apart from the paper. Good-quality unbleached linen tape or strips of vellum can usually be relied upon for permanence but the hemp cords and linen thread used in books bound a century ago has often deteriorated to a serious extent, resulting in loose sections and broken backs. On pulling such a book, the thread and cords are sometimes found to be too weak to be serviceable. Provided a careful examination is made before use, the materials of the present-day manufacture should be quite satisfactory as regards permanence. An unsatisfactory tape or cord will show signs of weakness when tested on a tensile testing machine. Since sewing materials play such a vital part in the durability of a book great care must be exercised when replacing the traditional materials by newer products, except in the case of certain modern synthetics, such as nylon and Terylene, which are so outstandingly good in many ways that there should be little risk in using them.

It is important to realize that there are many other synthetic fibres, some of which are suspect from their very nature. For example, threads and fabrics having a base of polyvinyl chloride or polyvinylidene chloride should be regarded with suspicion, as well as any other fibre containing highly chlorinated organic materials. Since it is difficult for the layman to be sure of detecting these materials, he should confine his choice to nylon and Terylene until the other synthetics have been tested more fully and found to be satisfactory. Tape made of nylon and Terylene should be as enduring as the threads made from these materials. Nearly all the synthetics are less affected by moisture than linen, hemp, etc. They do not lose strength to anything like the same extent as linen and, consequently, are less likely to shrink and cause an irritating slight ripple in the sections sewn with them. Silk thread has already a very high reputation for permanent bindings, but one serious objection to it is its habit of unravelling during use. This can be avoided in the same way as for nylon, i.e. by sizing with diluted P.V.A. emulsion. Since silk is an expensive material, the binder must be on the alert for inferior grades which can deteriorate even faster than over-bleached cotton. The best silk is that which has been processed as little as possible and the most durable kind of silk is known as "silk in the gum." Surgeons' ligature silk is generally of excellent quality and can be used with confidence, especially when its cost would be small in comparison with its importance in the finished book. It should be borne in mind that silk and nylon are sensitive to ultra-violet light and should never be used where they will be exposed unduly to strong sunlight; it is preferable to hide them away from it. If paste and glue are prepared with a small amount of inhibitor or fungicide, there is no need to treat threads, cords or tapes separately; they will absorb enough from the adhesives to make them immune. The synthetics should be naturally immune.

CHAPTER 8

ADHESIVES

UNTIL comparatively recently the whole question of adhesion was treated in an empirical manner. During the last few decades, however, a much more systematic development has been evident, probably because the new synthetic adhesives have been developed by firms with well-equipped research laboratories. The development has not yet gone far enough to place the subject on a scientific basis, but it has progressed far beyond the rule-of-thumb empiricism of a generation ago.

In the past, the bookbinder was content with two adhesives— starch paste and glue. Today, he can still prepare both these materials in a form good enough for permanent archive work, but if he wishes to use one of the multitude of ready-prepared pastes he is likely to be very much embarrassed by the enormous variety to choose from. The newer synthetics are, in most cases, so very different from the old-fashioned pastes and glues that, in the absence of guidance, he may be excused for avoiding them for permanent records.

Since the question of adhesives for archives is so important, and since the development of new adhesives is likely to be accelerated in the future, the following short general account of the principles of adhesion, as applied to adhesives, should give the archivist and bookbinder a sound background against which to judge present and future developments in this field.

The use of adhesives in bookbinding should be regarded as a necessary evil, on the principle that joints are potential sources of weakness. It is not so much that the adhesive itself may be weak but that the contact between it and the materials to be joined may be so. Furthermore, most adhesives dry to a hard, horny layer which, in the case of paper, will usually have an abrupt edge, thus, if the paper is bent it will, in all probability, bend sharply about this edge, concentrating most of the stress along it and causing it eventually to crack. This, perhaps, is the strongest argument against single-page binding, no matter how good the adhesive or how strong the paper.

Adhesives hold two paper surfaces together, either by mechanical or chemical binding or both. In mechanical binding, the adhesive is forced into minute undercut hollows in the surface of the paper to which it is applied and, on drying, these form hard dumb-bell-like anchors in the substance of the paper. This action can be rendered visible by suitable magnification of a cross-section of a glued paper or wood joint.

The chemical binding is rather more difficult to explain in simple terms, but it can be illustrated quite simply by applying thin paste to clean paper and to paper thoroughly impregnated with wax. The clean paper will be "wetted" by the paste while the waxed paper, with its chemically different surface, actually repels the paste. If the adhesive fulfils the requirements of both actions in a high degree it is likely to give a comparatively strong joint. This is seen in the case of two layers of paper properly pasted together when, after drying, the joint will be found to be stronger than the paper and, when torn apart, the break will be in the paper and not in the paste.

The first essential, therefore, of a good adhesive is that it shall wet the surfaces to be joined; otherwise the joint will be weak, as in the case of the joint between paste and wax. In order that the adhesive shall have a good chance of wetting the surfaces, assuming that it is capable of so doing, it must be fluid or plastic at some stage of making the joint. For example, if the glue in a joint is allowed to cool and set before the joint is made it will lose most of its adhesiveness and a weak joint will result.

However, once the two parts of the joint have been brought together, the quicker the glue sets the sooner the joint can be handled without damaging it, and the sooner the glue dries, the sooner the joint will reach its final strength. There should therefore be three stages in the setting of an adhesive: a fluid stage for free manipulation, a quick initial set after the joint has been brought into position, and a final set to reach maximum strength.

Practical adhesives vary greatly in their "sets," as regards both the time and the conditions under which they take place. Sometimes the initial set takes place by cooling, as with glue, sometimes by evaporation, as with paste. The final set, so far as adhesives used by the archivist are concerned, usually takes place by evaporation. This type of setting almost always results in shrinkage which, if severe, may cause the adhesive to shrink away from the surfaces of the joint and leave it weak or defective.

A further essential, though it is perhaps rather an academic point, is that the adhesive should itself be about as strong as the materials to be joined. For instance, wax will make a joint between two steel surfaces if applied hot and allowed to cool, but such a joint would be too weak to have much practical value owing to the comparative weakness of the wax.

Finally, if an adhesive makes the paper to which it is applied too wet, it can cause severe cockling, due to uneven or excessive expansion, and may give trouble on drying. If these considerations are borne in mind it should be easier to understand the properties of practical adhesives than it would otherwise have been.

STARCH PASTES

Starch paste may have been used by the Egyptians to join sheets of papyrus into long rolls; it is still one of the most commonly-used adhesives for paper. The obvious reason for this long vogue is that it satisfactorily fulfils the many practical requirements for an adhesive and does so cheaply.

Starch paste, especially in some of its modern modifications, has a wide range of useful properties as an adhesive for paper and leather and, though it may not allow of the speed of working possible with animal glues, it has the compensating advantage of greater convenience. If one part of almost any flour or, better still, starch is mixed with ten parts of water and heated to boiling point an excellent paste can be obtained. Provided it is used before gelling and reversion sets in and before active mould growth spoils it, it would be difficult to improve on this simple and inexpensive paste.

Most modern modifications are aimed at improving its flow qualities, by preventing or retarding the onset of gelling by preserving it against mouldiness and putrefaction or by increasing the resistance of the finished joint to moisture. It is useful, when departing from the simple paste, to keep these factors in mind and not accept extra trouble or cost which cannot be offset by some compensating advantage.

Industrial Paste Manufacture

Ready-made pastes are very attractive to the archivist. They can be made with an amazing variety of properties to cover a wide range of individual requirements and they save the trouble and mess involved in the home-made product. Against these advantages must be placed the disadvantages of extra cost, uncertainty of composition and possible unsuitability for permanent archive work. The following notes should give some idea of the range of commercial pastes available, with their good and bad points.

In industrial practice, the best pastes are made from starches and only the cheaper grades from the less pure flours. The flours contain much of the gluten of the grain or tuber from which they were made and, consequently, pastes made from them are much more liable to putrefaction than those made from the highly purified starches. Furthermore, the flours sometimes impart an undesirable colour to the paste. The starches most commonly used are tapioca, sago, corn (maize), white potato and, more recently, waxy maize and sweet potato. There is a strong family resemblance between them all, though they differ to a small extent and each has a field in which it best fulfils requirements.

If ten per cent pastes are made from any of these starches they will not differ much while still warm. On cooling, however, only the paste from rice starch and waxy maize will remain fluid for any length of time; the rest will set to gels at varying rates. If the paste is to be applied with a brush, the fluid condition is much more desirable and, consequently, with the gelling pastes it is usual to stir or beat them on cooling to break down the gel structure and render them more brushable. After gelling, most pastes shrink and exude a certain amount of clear liquid—the so-called reversion.

Natural starches are often modified to give pastes with special properties, usually an increase in the starch to water ratio. For example, if the starch is treated with either alkali, acid or oxidizing agents, it can be made much more soluble in water and the normal 1 to 10 ratio can be increased to as much as 1 to 1 without making the paste too stiff to work. Another very common method of achieving the same result is to roast the starch, either with a small amount of acid at moderate temperatures or without acid at higher temperatures, to produce the range of white and yellow dextrins and British gums. The latter, at the end of the range, are completely soluble in cold water and give clear solutions which are still fluid at a 1 to 1 ratio.

As a result of these treatments, a wide range of properties, apart from the starch to water ratio, can be made available. The tackiness, initial set, water sensitivity and spreading power can all be varied to suit the requirements of different spreading mechanisms and of the different materials to be joined. Any archivist, whose consumption of paste is sufficiently high to make it worth while, can have his special requirements catered for, often at moderate cost.

The small user who cannot expect to command this special treatment will usually have to make his own paste and there is no reason why he should not fare as well as the larger user. If he buys ready-made pastes he will have to take them without knowing whether they may contain excess acid, alkali, oxidizing agent or any of the many antiseptics and fungicides available to the paste-maker. In the section dealing with the practical aspect of small-scale paste-making, the preparation of a few representative pastes is described (*see* p. 78).

Home-Made Pastes

These home-made pastes can be given properties which are especially suitable for permanent archive work and can be used without the risk attending the use of commercial pastes. A few general remarks on home-made pastes might be of interest here. It is doubtful if anything can surpass well made starch paste for simplicity in preparation, cheapness and effectiveness for paper and leather. There is a fairly close chemical similarity between the cellulose of paper and the starch of the paste, while the water is an excellent medium for preparing the paper to receive the starch.

Acid is the arch-enemy of paper, affecting its durability perhaps more than any other single factor, while starch, owing to its less highly organized structure, seems to suffer less severely. For this reason, paste should not be made with alum or any other acid antiseptic or preservative. The effect of the alum is to break down the starch molecule sufficiently to enable a higher starch to water ratio to be reached. A much better way of doing this is to add white dextrine to a straight starch paste. A ratio of 1 to 1 can be reached in this way.

When paste is prepared every few days there should not be much need for an antiseptic. But for paste that is to last for a week or longer, pure phenol (carbolic acid) should be used. (It has a much more effective antiseptic action than alum.) This substance, even in its pure form (ice crystals), tends to turn pink; if this is objectionable it can be avoided by using an equal amount of salicylanilide in place of the phenol. One commercial form of salicylanilide is known as "Shirlan."

Practical bookbinders often use mixtures of paste and glue for certain purposes, chiefly because the paste slows down the initial set of the glue while the glue imparts tack and quicker initial set to the paste. If pastes are prepared with a small proportion of glue they revert much more slowly than unmixed pastes. Some of the

synthetics, such as methylcellulose and carboxymethycellulose
(C.M.C.), are superior to glue in this respect. Formulæ embodying
these suggestions are given on page 79.

Cold Water Starches

These are starches so modified as to give acceptable pastes on
merely mixing with cold water. They are used largely by paper-
hangers and decorators and are suitable for rough work generally.
They frequently consist of modified starches or starches gelatinized
by heating with a minimum amount of water: if the added water
is kept low enough the final product will remain in the form of a
loose powder while the bulk of the individual grains will be
burst and gelatinized. They give rather coarse-grained pastes
and, besides starch, may contain dextrins, other modified starches
and various antiseptics and modifying agents. They are undesirable for permanent archive work because of the uncertainty
of their composition, but for convenience they could hardly be
beaten.

GLUES AND GELATINES

Glues and gelatines are made from animal skins and bones. The
essential difference between the two lies in the greater purity of
the gelatine. Most glues and gelatines could be accommodated
in the range bounded by the very pure photographic gelatines at
the one end of the scale and by scotch glue at the other.

The skins used are generally the trimmings cut from the hides
and skins to be used for tanning. They are soaked in lime to
remove hair and then further soaked in strong limes until well
swollen, whereupon they are thoroughly washed in successive
lots of water, at increasing temperatures, until most of the lime
has been removed and systematically extracted. The liquors are
concentrated to the required strength and allowed to cool and set
to a jelly which is cut into sheets or slabs and dried in the air. The
best products come from the lowest temperature extraction.
When bones are used they are treated in dilute acids to remove the
mineral matter from them, after which they are treated in the
same way as the skins.

ALBUMEN

Albumen is usually made from slaughterhouse tankage (blood); it is in fact dried blood serum. It is not heated during its preparation so that it remains soluble in water.

CASEIN

Casein is the albumen extracted from milk. Milk is curdled by natural or artificial means and the curds, consisting largely of casein, are collected, dried at low temperature and ground to powder.

Only the glues are of much interest to the bookbinder and the archivist. The casein adhesives, so useful for wood, can only be made workable by adding fairly strong alkalis and this rules them out for use with paper and vellum. When these adhesives have dried and set they have the advantage of being rather less affected by moisture than glues. Albumen, too, is not used by the binder as an adhesive because it requires heat to set it. When set it also is less moisture-sensitive than the glues. Gelatine could be used in place of glue but, besides being more expensive, its initial set takes place too rapidly for convenience. Thus, in practice, glue is the only one of this class of animal adhesives which finds a use in archive work.

GENERAL PROPERTIES OF GLUES

The most useful properties of glues, from the bookbinder's point of view, are their moderately rapid initial set and high "solids to water" ratio. In practice, this means that the binder can work much faster using glue than he can when using paste, since he can handle glued joints very soon after making them. The high solids ratio means that cockling is reduced to a minimum.

Although paste can usually replace glue when time is not important, glue has a special value for rounding and backing because it passes through a plastic range just before becoming air dry. This gives the glued spine of a book a very convenient malleability, facilitates the rounding and reduces the liability to "starts."

Thin hot glue has a greater power of penetration into paper than paste, a property which gives it a better mechanical hold by the "dumb-bell" effect. The high solids ratio enables glue to fill the gap between poorly fitting surfaces, a distinct advantage when carefully surfaced joints are not possible.

All glues consist of gelatine more or less modified by heating and more or less contaminated by non-gelatine from the skin, bones, etc., used in their manufacture. Good glue can be made from either skin or bones and it would be a very poor glue indeed that would not be strong enough for joining paper, boards, leather and other bookbinding materials. Generally speaking glue, if used correctly, has mechanically much greater strength than the binder can possibly need, but it saves time.

Gelatine is the constituent responsible for the malleability of glue and, usually, the higher the proportion of gelatine in a glue the shorter is the time of initial set and the sooner the joint can be handled. At the same time, a high gelatine glue can set too rapidly and require great skill in handling if weak joints are to be avoided. Repeated heating of glue, as often happens to the glue in a gluepot which is not being frequently replenished and cleaned out, will degrade the gelatine and lengthen the time of initial set and may ultimately give an adhesive with little more set than paste.

Small amounts of acid and alkali are used in glue manufacture but are generally removed before the glue comes on the market. Modern glues are often sold in pearls, cubes or powder. The use of these forms, provided that the glue itself is of good quality, is to be strongly recommended because they soften and swell rapidly in cold water and melt smoothly without prolonged heating.

A very satisfactory glue for bookbinders is a light coloured cabinet maker's glue. This is rather high in gelatine and may set too rapidly for some purposes; this is easily remedied by adding a little phenol (carbolic acid) which has the added advantage of preserving the glue and rendering it somewhat less palatable to insect and other pests.

Flexible glues are often used by the binder, especially for the less important books where the glue remains as the "backing." They are usually ordinary glues containing glycerine or, according to more modern usage, sorbitol. The softening effect of the latter substance, which is prepared from sugar, is supposed to last longer than that of glycerine but it is doubtful whether flexible glues are really required for the most durable bindings. It should be borne in mind that these softening agents, "humectants," owe their efficacy to the fact that they absorb moisture from the air and, in extreme cases, they may absorb so much that there will be a risk of mould growth on the glue, even under such abnormal conditions, unless sufficient antiseptic has been added to prevent this happening.

There are a number of ways of lowering the setting temperature of glues and it is possible to carry the lowering to the stage where the glues remain liquid at room temperature. Where large surfaces have to be glued and sound joints are essential, as, for example, in building up the laminated wood airplane propellers, the time of initial set must be lengthened for practical reasons. A special glue containing cresol has proved itself to be very satisfactory for this purpose for, though it is not liquid at room temperatures, it has a very low melting point and correspondingly long setting time.

In addition, the use of cresol, or other phenol of this type, acts as an effective antiseptic and enables the glue to be marketed with the correct amount of water and ready for use after gentle warming. Such glues would be satisfactory for the binder though they might not be as good as the acetic acid glues for rounding since they seem to have a rather short range of malleability.

Acetic acid glues can be made to remain liquid at room

temperatures but since this involves the use of rather an excessive amount of acetic acid a convenient compromise is to use sufficient to give a glue which sets at about 60°F.

Acetic acid is not sufficiently strong to damage paper and it disappears during the drying, leaving a more or less normal glue behind. This glue gives satisfactory results for rounding and backing and is well worth a trial; it is liquid at the usual workshop temperatures and avoids the necessity for the conventional gluepot which is hardly a practical proposition for the small binder who only occasionally needs glue.

The acetic acid content will slowly corrode the tin-plate and copper of brushes so care should be taken to wash these after use. It might also affect the colour of some papers and linens; these materials should, therefore, be tested before the glue is used. The gluepot is a "messy" piece of apparatus, except where it is in constant use by a careful worker, and, with a little ingenuity, it should be possible to dispense with the need for glue, except for rounding and backing and for some rather open-textured linens.

VEGETABLE GLUES AND GLUE SUBSTITUTES

Some starch adhesives, such as yellow dextrins and British gums, can be dissolved in water to give a high enough "solids to water" ratio to justify their use as a substitute for glue in certain cases. They lack the rapid and clear-cut initial set of glue but, with some practice, they can be made to give fairly satisfactory results and they offer the great advantage of always being ready for instant use, thus avoiding the need for the gluepot. As the making of these special pastes will be rather beyond the capacity of the ordinary binder's workshop, the commercial products will normally have to be used and this raises the difficulty of deciding whether they contain anything likely to be detrimental to permanent archives.

MISCELLANEOUS ADHESIVES

The adhesives listed here are, generally, of rather more limited value to the bookbinder than glue or paste.

Gum Arabic

Solutions of gum arabic in water have long been used as adhesives for paper. They are not of much interest to the book-binder, though the archivist may occasionally come across them. Their chief use is for postage stamps and general office purposes. They produce clear, easy brushing solutions which have no marked initial set but pass through a tacky stage on drying. The properties for which they are most prized are ready solution in water after drying, so that stamps and envelope flaps only need moistening to give good and rapid adhesion, and their agreeable flavour. They will normally be too "moisture sensitive" for permanent work, though their readiness for immediate use, cleanliness and ease of application with a brush make them convenient for less important documents. They have an advantage over the cheaper British gums of not becoming sticky on exposure to a moist atmosphere.

Gum Strip

These modern string substitutes have recently become popular for sealing packages and similar rough jobs for which they are very suitable. They are not likely to be used for archives though there are many unimportant uses to which they may be put. Like all "re-moistening" adhesives they are necessarily moisture sensitive and joints made with them can readily be unmade by moistening them with water, though not with non-aqueous solvents.

Rubber Adhesives

Rubber solutions in naphtha or carbon tetrachloride are sometimes used as temporary adhesives for paper and cardboard. On drying, the film of rubber which remains has a small holding power, often good enough for certain purposes. Their chief advantage is that the film of rubber can readily be rubbed or pulled off, when it has served the temporary need, without damaging the surface of the paper or cardboard. Their chief interest to the bookbinder is a historical one. About 1880, rubber "solution" was used as the adhesive for single-sheet bindings, which showed signs of becoming popular about this time, because of its cheapness and the very agreeable flexibility of the bound book.

Unfortunately, the rubber gradually perished and, after a few years, the books became piles of loose sheets again. Most libraries still have some examples of these epitaphs to the bookbinder's optimism. This single-sheet binding—the so-called "perfect" binding—is being revived at the present time using the modern synthetic adhesive polyvinyl acetate in place of rubber. These bindings are less likely to fail through the perishing of the adhesive but are just as likely to do so through other inherent weaknesses. They will be mentioned again when synthetic adhesives are being considered.

Synthetic Adhesives

Modern synthetic adhesives are a somewhat numerous class and, although they have mostly been advocated for joints where waterproofness is important, they are in general less convenient to use and more expensive than glues and pastes.

The occasions on which the adhesive used in bookbinding is likely to be called upon to withstand actual wetting are extremely rare and may in normal practice be disregarded, although there are cases of stores of valuable books being under water due to fire or the bursting of water mains, when the use of a more water- and rot-proof adhesive than glue might possibly have saved them. However, as paper itself is neither waterproof nor water-resistant, the binder will probably find glue and paste more satisfactory for his purpose, unless the more expensive adhesive has something other than mere waterproofness to offer.

In this connexion, it is important not to lose sight of the fact that great strength in an adhesive cannot in most cases be used to advantage since the materials to be joined have a low tensile strength and a joint will break at its weakest point. So long as the adhesive is a little stronger than the material to be joined, there is nothing to be gained from strengthening it further. With these facts in mind the newer adhesives can be separated fairly definitely into the satisfactory and the unsatisfactory.

Most of the modern plastics and polymers fall conveniently into one of two categories: they are either thermo-plastic or thermo-setting. The differences are deep-seated and each category has its own field of usefulness. The thermo-setting plastics, in their final state, are generally infusible at temperatures up to the charring point and are insoluble in solvents. The great majority of these materials are made either from phenol and formaldehyde or from urea and formaldehyde. The urea is nowadays sometimes replaced by melamine.

They are much used for mouldings where heat and pressure can be used for setting them. Once set, they can only be shaped by cutting, they no longer become plastic on heating and they are, for all practical purposes, insoluble in solvents. Before reaching the final stage, however, they can be used as adhesives for ply-wood, for which purpose they have largely supplanted the older glue, casein or albumen adhesives. The phenolic resin bonded plywood can withstand some years of exposure in the open air in England without exfoliation, while samples buried in soil have rotted away leaving the adhesive behind. The urea and melamine resins are used for similar purposes.

The objection to both these types of resin for archive work is that they require a dangerously high acidity to set them at low temperatures in a reasonable time. Unless considerable changes are made in their properties these plastics should not be used for archive work.

Polyester and epoxy resins are a more recent development in this field and may have more to offer the archivist when they have had longer to settle down into their different fields of application. For the present, therefore, all the thermo-setting resins should be regarded as essentially "heavy duty" adhesives, more suitable for use with wood and metals than with paper and leather.

The thermo-plastics are a much more varied class and have some interest for the archivist. These, like the thermo-setting resins, are ploymers but they can be softened at moderate temperatures to become plastic and mouldable and are usually soluble in various solvents. Most of these plastics are horny or rubbery solids and, when mixed with a suitable solvent or plasticizer, become sticky and develop adhesive properties. It would hardly be possible to give even a summary of this numerous class of materials. There are a few of them, however, which have shown themselves to have a real interest for the archivist.

The most interesting of these is polyvinyl acetate, especially in the emulsion form. Of all the modern synthetics, this, so far, seems to hold out the most hope of competing with the more conventional starch and glue adhesives for paper and leather. It can be given a wide variety of attractive properties and, so far as can be judged at present, should be as permanent as the archivist could reasonably demand. It is a clear, water-white, horny solid which softens when heated to rather less than the boiling point of water. By the addition of a small amount of plasticizer, such as dibutyl phthalate, it becomes first rubbery and then tacky. It could be used in solution in a non-aqueous solvent but in this form it is much too viscous for most purposes and, if thinned down sufficiently, would have a very low solids content.

The emulsion form is the most interesting; it may have a solid to liquid ratio as high as glue and still be fluid enough to work easily under the brush. Modern P.V.A. emulsions are becoming deservedly popular for bookbinding; the more rubbery ones make excellent flexible adhesives for the spine of a book. One of the advantages of P.V.A. in emulsion form is that it can be diluted with water and is always ready for immediate use. When dry, the film of P.V.A. remaining in the joint is fairly waterproof and rotproof. The rubbery form seems likely to preserve its flexibility indefinitely at ordinary temperatures.

Before drying, adhesion can be effected without pressure and, even after drying, P.V.A.-treated surfaces can be made to adhere by warmth or pressure. One great advantage of P.V.A. is that it is a good adhesive for silk, nylon and Terylene fibres and fabrics, for which glue and paste are not very satisfactory. Since it is less affected than paper by water, some care should be taken to deal with curling if it is used on one side of the paper only.

An important practical difficulty in using the emulsion is that it quickly gums up the fibres of any brush on which it is allowed to dry. The only remedy for this is to dissolve out the P.V.A. with methylated spirits or one of the lacquer solvents, such as acetone or ethyl acetate which should always be kept handy in case of accidents. The gumming up of brushes can be avoided by keeping a jar of water handy and by putting the brushes into it after use. Once this habit has been acquired it becomes second nature and enables brushes used for P.V.A. emulsion to have a more normal life.

Pressure-Sensitive Tapes

These are usually thin, transparent viscose (cellophane) ribbons with a permanently tacky adhesive on one side. They stick with great tenacity to almost anything solid immediately they make contact with it. So far as archives are concerned, they are usually a nuisance and the archivist's chief concern is to remove them without removing the surface of the paper at the same time. This can be done by applying a small amount of a solvent, such as methylated spirit or carbon tetrachloride, to one edge of the tape, raising this edge as soon as it is free and allowing more solvent to flow into the opening thus made. Gradually the tape should yield and then, with more solvent on a plug of cotton-wool, the paper should be sponged until free from sticky adhesive.

PRACTICAL WORKSHOP DATA

The preparation of starch pastes in small amounts needs a certain amount of precision if unexpected results are to be avoided. Small cheap spring balances, sufficiently accurate for this type of work, are sold by stationers for office use; one taking a maximum load of 24 oz and graduated in eighths of an ounce will be satisfactory for most of these small paste-making operations. A liquid measure, similar to those used by cooks and graduated in fractions of a pint, can usually be obtained from any domestic hardware shop.

General Remarks on Paste-making

The traditional way of making paste is to mix the starch with enough water to give a thin smooth cream and then to add boiling water rapidly, with vigorous stirring. Stirring is important if the paste is not to become lumpy as lumps, once formed, are difficult to break down. The paste so obtained may be allowed to cool until set and then well stirred or beaten smooth to break down the gel structure. Alternatively, the hot paste may be boiled in a thick-bottomed pan or a double saucepan for 5–30 minutes to complete the swelling and bursting of the starch granules. The extra boiling usually gives a much smoother and more uniform paste.

When using dextrins as additions to the straight starch paste, it should be remembered that these, especially the white dextrins, have rather variable characteristics. But all of them dissolve readily in hot water to give comparatively thinly fluid solutions.

A good general utility paste can be made as follows—

Corn starch.	4 oz
Water	2 pints
*Antiseptic Mix	$\frac{5}{8}$ oz

These ingredients should be heated to boiling and be well stirred during heating. On cooling the paste should be stirred or beaten with a flat piece of wood or wooden spoon to break down the gel structure. This paste should keep indefinitely if evaporation is prevented.

The above paste is white, brushes easily when freshly prepared and, even when set, is not troublesome to brush out. It does,

---

* The amount of the pure unmixed antiseptic required to make this amount of paste may be inconveniently small to weigh accurately. In this formula it is mixed with starch to make it heavier and so easier to weigh accurately. If larger batches are to be made the pure Shirlan could be used, when only one-third of the above amount would be needed.

Soluble Shirlan	4 oz
Starch	8 oz

however, revert after some days' standing but, even in this condition, it works fairly satisfactorily under the brush. Its reversion can be retarded by adding small amounts of glue, or better still, methyl cellulose to the above ingredients. A normal amount of these materials to be added to the above formula is half an ounce. If glue in powder form is used, it can be mixed with the starch cream before the addition of the boiling water. If pearl or lump glue is used it must be fully swollen in cold water, before adding to the starch cream. The methyl cellulose should be mixed with the dry starch after both have been weighed out. The methyl cellulose makes a very attractive paste and well justifies its extra trouble and expense, especially for repair work.

If pastes with high "solids to water" ratio are required, white dextrins can be added to the formula for straight starch paste. The dextrin is preferably mixed with the dry starch before creaming. Any quantity up to three or even four times the weight of starch can be used. These modifications of the straight starch paste should meet almost all the normal requirements of the archivist and bookbinder.

Glues

When glue is required in small quantities only or at infrequent intervals, the usual gluepot is not a very practical tool. There is much to be said for making up the glue and keeping it in a closed wide-mouthed bottle. When required for use, the glue can be melted by standing the bottle in hot water but, unless some antiseptic is used, even when the bottle is well closed, the glue jelly is likely to turn mouldy.

Glue brushes used infrequently are difficult to soften if they have meanwhile dried out, and if they are left in the solid glue it will hardly be possible to keep the bottle closed. Brushes should, therefore, be washed in hot water after use or should be kept, bristles downward, in a bottle with just about the right sized mouth to make a close fit with the handle of the brush.

Since thick glue is not often wanted and is always difficult and risky to use, the following formula was designed to give a thin glue when hot—soak 5 oz of glue in 10 oz of cold water till swollen and add ¼ oz of phenol. A small amount of phenol in the finished glue prevents mould growth indefinitely and slightly lengthens the time of initial set. Pale cabinet maker's glue is suggested as giving a suitable compromise of properties. Glue in the form of pearls is now generally available; it should be used if possible since it swells fairly rapidly in cold water (about 1–2 hours) and its colour and freedom from contamination with dirt can easily be judged by the eye.

Glues containing this antiseptic mix should preferably not be used in iron or steel containers but only in glass, enamelled iron or stainless steel. If the ordinary gluepot is to be used the antiseptic should be excluded.

Liquid Glues

Phenol or cresol added to glue lengthens its time of initial set. The addition of 5 per cent of phenol based on the weight of the glue, i.e. ¼ oz to the above ingredients, is a suitable amount to be used. Excellent commercial glues of this type can be purchased in small quantities in lever-top tins from ironmongers and it is usually more satisfactory to buy them ready made. They are not likely to contain any harmful ingredients. However, experience and judgment are demanded if they are used for rounding and backing and this suggests that they may have a much narrower range of malleability than plain glues.

The liquid glues made with acetic acid seem to be quite suitable for general use, provided they are not allowed to remain long in contact with metals. The following formula is for a glue which sets at about 60°F. It is liquid above this temperature and solid below it. At a few degrees above the setting point it is like a thick glue and could be used for the more open-wove linens.

Pearl glue	.	. 4 oz
Water	.	. 6 oz
Glacial acetic acid		. 2 oz
Antiseptic mix		. ⅛ oz (*see* page 78)

A wide-mouthed bottle with moulded screw cap is suitable for this liquid glue provided that the thread is wiped dry before replacing the cap.

Polyvinyl Acetate Emulsions

The usual thick emulsion, as purchased, should be well stirred with a clean wooden stick before use in order to mix the thick sediment which falls to the bottom of the container. In most uses the emulsion is rather too thick for convenient usage and $1\frac{1}{2}$ pints of it should be well mixed with $\frac{1}{2}$ pint of water. The weaker emulsion is much more convenient to use with a brush than the strong emulsion.

For sizing nylon or Terylene thread, $\frac{1}{2}$ pint of thick emulsion (as received) should be mixed with $1-1\frac{1}{2}$ pints of water. The hanks of thread are allowed to soak in this dilute emulsion for a few minutes, removed and hung up to drip and dry in the air. The degree of sizing can be controlled by varying the amount of water added to the thick emulsion.

All these emulsions, whether thick or thin, should always be stirred before use; otherwise they will tend to settle out and leave a weaker emulsion on top and a thicker emulsion underneath. For this reason, it is a useful practical precaution to keep a small amount of emulsion separate from the bulk for immediate use and to replenish this from the stock as and when required. A wide-mouthed bottle with a moulded screw cap is suitable, provided the screw threads of the bottle are wiped dry before replacing the cap.

CHAPTER 9

OTHER BOOKBINDING MATERIALS

ALTHOUGH the less important bookbinding materials do not play a vital role in the permanence of the book, their failure may necessitate repairs which would weaken the book at a later date.

BOARDS

Since the old rope board is now very difficult to obtain commercially a good quality of mill board makes a good "second best." Mill boards are in general less tough and stiff than rope boards but the difference only becomes apparent with large books or when a book is dropped on its corner in use. Straw board, the third alternative, is a poor substitute, being mechanically weak in all directions. It has been used in the past for cheap machine-bound books and appears to be chemically very permanent. Perhaps the best boards are those which the bookbinder can himself make by pasting together sheets of brown wrapping paper, pressing and drying them. Such boards, made from good Kraft wrapping paper with plenty of paste and pressure, are rigid, hard and tough and are often well worth the trouble involved in their preparation. The author's experience of boards from old books stripped for rebinding suggests that there is little to choose between any of them as regards permanence. Even old straw board, which one would expect to have the shortest life of all, shows no obvious sign of deterioration with age. Probably a hundred years is not long enough to enable one to decide how far one board material is better than another. Since boards and paper are made from similar materials—mill board is, indeed, sometimes made from repulped paper—it is surprising that the great variation in permanence shown by different papers is not reflected in board materials. This may be due to the fact that paper is almost always used in a highly bleached state while boards are usually made from unbleached material. Bleaching may possibly remove some naturally occurring inhibitor.

Recent work on the permanence of paper suggests that the rope board, though tough and strong initially, contains sufficient iron impurity to accumulate sulphuric acid from a contaminated atmosphere and consequently to lose strength in much the same way as paper under similar conditions but, of course, much more slowly. It has also been shown, rather surprisingly, that straw board should be very much less likely to suffer from this kind of deterioration than the mill boards at present available to the binder. Mill board, besides this supposed disadvantage, often suffers from a further defect from the binder's point of view, namely excessive lamination due, probably, to the pressure used in sheeting it. Straw board, while much weaker mechanically, is much less laminated and less liable to split or open out on handling; if its weakness to bending stresses could be removed, it would be preferable for permanent bindings. From a purely mechanical point of view, the bending of a sheet of material, such as a board, results in the maximum stretching and compression at the outer surfaces and if these could be stiffened the whole board would become much more rigid. This can easily be done by pasting hard, strong brown paper on both sides of the board; such a composite board is both light and stiff, is free from excessive lamination and is easily made. Two thicknesses of good Kraft paper on each side of the straw board are usually sufficient to stiffen a board finishing $\frac{1}{8}$ in. thick.

COVERING MATERIALS

The standard coverings for books which are bound to last are tanned goat skin and vellum. The lasting quality of vellum has been discussed in Chapter 5 and no more need be said here except that since vellum lacks the suppleness of leather it must be used with this consideration in mind. For covering the sides of a book it is ideal, except for its tendency to swell and shrink with changes in its moisture content. A marked change, either in the direction of increased dryness or of increased moistness, may produce warping of the boards which might or might not correct itself on returning to more normal conditions of humidity. The resistance of vellum to wear by attrition is probably higher than that of any other normally used covering material, while its durability, even in a sulphurous atmosphere, is excellent, owing possibly to the absence of catalytic metals and the presence of a reserve of alkali. It is likely to be much freer from traces of the dangerous metals, copper manganese and iron, than is leather. It is the use of vellum for the spine of a book which calls attention to its inferior suppleness in comparison with leather. Normally, vellum is too expensive to use as a covering and leather is used almost universally for high-class work.

LEATHER

Leather occupies a unique position among the covering materials used by the binder. Its interwoven, tough fibrous structure gives it a very desirable softness and strength while its chemical nature gives it the property of adhering well to paper, boards, linen and cellulosic materials in general, through the medium of glue and paste. In this respect, it is very much superior to many of the so-called imitation leathers and leather cloths. Leather, since it is a natural product obtained from a large variety of animals, is inevitably a highly variable material and when, in addition to this, the utmost skill of the tanner is brought to bear on it, it is not surprising that the varieties of leather on the market baffle description by the layman. The bookbinder should, therefore, buy his skins only from a reliable dealer or tanner and limit his choice to the few varieties which have been well tested over many years. But, quite apart from the ever increasing skill and in-genuity of the tanner, the ingenuity of the research chemist has recently been exercised in finding out how to prolong the life of leather. The whole story would require too long to recount here but, if the bookbinder is to feel confident enough to use leather for such vital duties as the lining or covering of books built to last, he should understand why leather has until recently earned its reputation for poor durability.

The Royal Society of Arts and the British Museum have both published information on the permanence of leather for book-binding and for fuller details these authorities should be consulted. In general terms, the permanence of leather, provided it is soundly preserved according to good modern practice, depends chiefly on the activity of certain catalytic metals, such as iron and copper, which find their way into leather as impurities during manufacture. Even the minute traces of these metals normally occurring in leather are sufficient to convert the sulphur dioxide in the air of industrial districts into sulphuric acid which remains fixed in the leather and may accumulate until it reaches five per cent of the weight of the leather, or even more. At this concentration of acid, leather rapidly disintegrates to dust and produces the familiar red rot of leather-covered books. This destruction could be prevented by protecting the book from contact with a sulphurous atmosphere by, for example, conditioning the air surrounding the books or by adding something to the leather which would, in effect, destroy the catalytic action of these metals. This, in fact, is the method recently advocated and to do this the leather is impregnated with a small percentage of disodium pyrophosphate. Previously, potassium lactate or citrate were used for this purpose but it is believed that pyrophosphate is more effective. It now seems possible that a good, modern tanned goatskin will be as permanent as vellum, even in a contaminated urban atmosphere, and, for the first time since polluted air has been the normal atmosphere surrounding a book, the suppleness of leather can be fully exploited for binding where cost is of secondary importance.

LINEN AND BUCKRAM

Librarians in the London area could show inquirers large numbers of books bound in half morocco with the leather crumbling to dust and the linen cloth or buckram in good condition even after a century of use. This demonstration should not be taken entirely at its face value. The modern proofing of leather might well give an entirely different result and a book bound with the best modern leathers and the best textile materials, would probably show both coverings in good condition and still mechanically sound a hundred years later. The chief mechanical difference between leather and the textiles used for covering lies in the arrangement of the fibres in each. A woven textile has its individual fibres interwoven in two dimensions, that is in one plane only, whereas leather has its fibres interwoven not only across the surface but also throughout its entire thickness. This difference partly explains the superiority of leather for withstanding certain kinds of wear and, to some extent, dictates the most suitable function for each type of material. In general terms, the suppleness and closeness of leather makes it an almost ideal material for the spine of a book where these properties can be used to the full. On the sides and edges of the boards, however, it withstands frictional wear less well than some of the textile materials, especially when these are treated with suitable impregnating or sizing materials to improve an already good resistance to attrition. The improvement is offset by a material reduction in the flexibility and suppleness of the fabric but, on the sides and edges of a book, this loss is much more than offset by the gain. In other words, each material ought to be used where it can be of the greatest service. This argument plainly suggests that full or half leather bindings are less likely to possess the durability of a quarter leather binding. Certainly, where durability alone is to be considered, the quarter binding is to be recommended, provided suitable leather and textiles are to be used. The usual textiles, linen and buckram, are excellent for this purpose, as the durability of certain bindings shows, but for first-class work something even better should be aimed at. It is true that these materials have not quite such a vital function to fulfil as those used for the spine of a book; nevertheless, their destruction may well call for a partial rebinding and this otherwise unnecessary operation is not likely to improve the other parts of the binding. A certain amount of work has been done with an unbleached linen fabric (tailor's canvas) impregnated with gelatine and this promises to give a material, for covering the sides and edges of boards, which combines many very desirable properties. The linen base is made from one of the most durable fibres known; and the material has been processed to the minimum extent so that the possibility of chemical damage has been reduced to negligible proportions. Its fibrous structure forms an ideal reinforcing medium for the tough horny gelatine, while the gelatine gives the fabric a very desirable surface hardness and resistance to attrition. It is easily worked by simply moistening and it takes glue and paste admirably. It has an attractive appearance when cut at 45° to the warp and its colour blends well with almost any colour of leather.

The relative values of the different leathers and of tanning and tawing (alum tannage) have been assessed by Cockerell and his book should be consulted for fuller details.

LEATHER SUBSTITUTES

Of the many substitutes for leather, proposed and manufactured, only two have any very extended use today. Both have a fabric base: one uses nitrocellulose as a covering while the other uses polyvinyl chloride. The first of these, which is commonly called Rexine from one of the earliest commercial forms, will always suffer from the defects of the nitrocellulose covering, which is rather hard and probably not very permanent. It is difficult to mould the Rexine to any but simple shapes and its chief value is for furniture where its good resistance to wear recommends it.

Polyvinyl chloride (P.V.C.) is suspect from its high chlorine content which might give rise to traces of hydrochloric acid over the long periods of time envisaged by the bookbinder. Apart from this, it is almost impossible to cause it to adhere to anything by any ordinary means. If some adhesive could be found which would be effective between polyvinyl chloride and other bookbinding materials and if the liability to decompose could be prevented, the material, which has a pleasant rubbery feel and extremely good resistance to frictional wear, would be interesting.

Furthermore, it is waterproof though the fabric base is certainly not. On the whole, it is much better to avoid these substitutes altogether. Some modern synthetics, apart from their use as constituents of leather cloth, can be used for impregnating textile materials in much the same way as was previously described for tailor's canvas/gelatine. Cellulose acetate and ethyl cellulose lend themselves to this use; in sufficient quantities they render the fabric comparatively waterproof and if resistance to moisture is deemed desirable for one reason or another, this is their chief advantage over gelatine. However, gelatine is more compatible with textiles, cheaper and probably much more durable than any of the plastics mentioned while it probably has an equally good resistance to attrition. A further disadvantage of the plastics is that they demand expensive solvents, many of which are not desirable in a bookbinder's workshop. Some plastics may contain traces of iron and, more probably, copper and are in addition not completely water resistant so that impermanence, operating from similar causes to that in paper, may arise. The remedy is similar though, if none of the common inhibitors is compatible, it may be necessary to use one of the modern acid-absorbing "epoxide" compositions.

Tailor's canvas impregnated with ethyl cellulose dissolved in benzene gives a result very similar in appearance to the tailors' canvas/gelatine fabrics previously described. It should also be more resistant to handling and is suitable for use where this quality is important and where permanence of a high order is not required.

PRACTICAL WORKSHOP DATA

Although reasonably permanent siding materials are available commercially special books may justify the trouble of preparing home-made linens.

Impregnation of Linen Fabric

Unbleached linen tailor's canvas—not hair cloth—is a strong fabric of simple weave and moderate stiffening. Many other strong-woven linen fabrics are available but tailor's canvas is particularly suitable for permanent binding and it can usually be bought retail at most linen draper's shops at a moderate price. The canvas is more convenient to impregnate if it is cut into strips and rolled into a loose cylinder. In this form it will fit conveniently into a jug or other more or less cylindrical vessel. A useful width for the strips is 6 in. or 12 in., depending on the depth of the jug or other vessel to be used. They may be cut parallel to the warp or at 45° to it. They are then loosely rolled into a cylinder ready for impregnation. Three yards of canvas 27 in. wide will make a cylindrical roll of 12 in. long by about 3 in. diameter. The container for the impregnating solution should not be much larger than is necessary to accommodate the roll, or a large amount of solution will be required, much of which may be wasted. The solution contains—

Pale skin glue or gelatine . 6 oz
Water . . . . 2 pints

Allow the glue to swell thoroughly in the water and heat in a jacketed vessel until the solution is thoroughly hot and all the glue is dissolved. The gelatine solution imparts somewhat less colour to the finished canvas but is rather more liable, when used in a cold workshop, to set before the impregnation is complete. The addition of a few drops of Stergene will shorten the time of impregnation but is not really necessary. The addition of $\frac{1}{2}$ oz of disodium pyrophosphate would make the permanence of the canvas more certain but should not be necessary, especially if this salt is added to the paste used for siding. Enough solution should be prepared to fill the impregnation vessel to a depth rather greater than the height of the roll (6 in. or 12 in.). The roll is then placed in the empty jug and the hot solution poured in until the roll is well covered. More solution should be added to replace that absorbed by the roll so that it is kept completely immersed. Impregnation should be completed in 15–20 minutes. The solution is then poured off and the roll allowed to drain for a few minutes, opened out and the separate strips pinned up separately by one edge and allowed to dry in the air. The fabric should be thoroughly soaked and dripping—the more glue that can be persuaded to stay in the fabric the better. When almost dry, the strips may be pressed flat. The impregnated fabric can be softened to almost any desired extent for working by moistening and may be fixed in place with either glue or paste. It does not shrink markedly on drying.

Hardening Solution for Impregnated Canvas

When the canvas is in position on the book and thoroughly dry it is advantageous to harden it by sponging it lightly with a plug of cotton wool wet with the following solution—

Alcohol (methylated spirit) .	1 pint
Tannic Acid　　.　　.	. 2 oz
Water　　.　　.　　.	. 0–2 oz

The water helps the alcohol to dissolve the tannic acid, but only a minimum amount should be used and, in some cases, none at all may be necessary.

The solution dries rapidly and the fabric can then be given a smoother and more pleasant feel by sponging it over with a 10 per cent solution of shellac in spirit. Although this series of operations sounds complicated it is quite simple once the materials are available and the technique is mastered. The final result is pleasant to look at, agreeable to the touch, extremely resistant to wear and soiling and probably as durable as any other material composing the book. It is, however, rather too rough to take lettering very satisfactorily. The other forms of fabric covering tend to be thinner, less durable and less pleasant in appearance but are available in a condition ready for use and are cheaper than the prepared tailor's canvas. Generally, unless permanence is the overriding consideration, the question of cost will decide which covering should be used.

CHAPTER 10

BINDING TECHNIQUES

A WELL-BOUND book, the product of sound materials and good craftsmanship, is surprisingly durable considering the softness of its component materials. This durability can only be attained when all the materials used are compatible with each other and equally durable. The careless use of water-repellent materials in combination with water-absorbing paper, leather, etc., may cause mechanical instability of the whole book. Adhesives, threads, etc., which lose their strength in use would have the same effect. Compatibility of materials, therefore, is an important factor in durability. In cases where the good sense and experience of the craftsman can be relied upon to make a wise choice of materials, a well-balanced book will result.

Nevertheless, it often happens that traditional materials become scarce or modern processes of manufacture turn out a product inferior in stability to the material to which the craftsman is accustomed. Furthermore, new materials are constantly being produced and the craftsman is often at a loss to know to what extent he can trust them. His usual criterion is to avoid using untried material until it has been used for less important work over a sufficient period to enable him to judge of its suitability for his own purpose.

These considerations raise the question of accelerated ageing tests which are the only alternative to waiting a generation or so before using a new material. These tests may not always be reliable, occasionally giving an unduly optimistic or pessimistic view, but in general they are not likely to give a wholly false view, provided always that the test has been devised by someone skilled in such work and that the results are accepted with reasonable reserve. They are, in fact, the only safeguard against such

91

mistakes as were made in the period 1880–90 when rubber solution was used as the adhesive for the spines of books. After a few years of normal storage and use the rubber perished and the books, in many cases, fell to pieces. A simple ageing test would have prevented this and sounded a note of warning to the craftsmen who were attracted to the delightful flexibility of the books bound by the agency of rubber adhesive.

Having considered the limitations of constructive materials, there remains still the question of the *technique* of the binder. The position here is comparatively simple. The medieval binder evolved methods and processes which have stood the test of time and, provided the same degree of skill is acquired by the modern binder, through practice and training, equally good results should be obtained. It must be obvious, however, that the established techniques are expensive and time consuming and do not, to any great extent, lend themselves to mechanical treatment. It would be too reactionary to assert that these old methods could not be improved upon; they could certainly be cheapened with only a slightly adverse effect upon stability and durability.

New materials, if otherwise satisfactory, often demand a change in the method of use and, for this and for many other reasons, the technique of the bookbinder must change gradually with the passage of time if it is not to become hidebound and moribund. For a valuable book the nearest approach to the traditional methods of the old binders will always be called for, since here the cost will not be a serious consideration, in view of the value of the finished book, and since such work will always create a confidence which the use of new materials and technique cannot hope to do.

A very good example of the kind of change in technique which might result is seen in the use of the new synthetic fibres. These have not only much greater tensile strength than traditional fibres but seem to resist breakdown from repeated bending. These properties, if confirmed, suggest that the sections of a book could be hinged to guards, instead of being bound into the spine by traditional methods, while the guards could be sewn, rounded and backed in the usual way.

This treatment not only gives greatly increased flexibility to a stiff paper section but, doubtless at the same time, reduces the stresses due to flexing of the paper near the back of the pages. Furthermore, by cutting the threads at the hinge between section and guard, the section could be freed in a condition undamaged by the usual rounding and backing operations, in case rebinding becomes necessary. However, while such treatment is gentle to the section, it throws additional stress on the thread which, unless it is capable of standing this, will be a source of mechanical instability.

A less commendable example of the effect of new materials on technique recalls the use of rubber solution in the binding of single sheets. The discovery and production of flexible polyvinyl acetate (P.V.A.) adhesives has recently revived single-sheet binding, with some advantage over the old rubber process, in that P.V.A. is less likely to perish, but still saddled with the inherent defect of mechanically weak pages, a weakness of the paper used in this way rather than of the adhesive. Even if the adhesive remained tenacious and flexible for a thousand years the paper would flex at the "glue line" and would soon become so weak that it would tear, even with gentle handling. It is the technique here which is inherently bad.

GUARDING

This operation has been very fully described by Cockerell and, since good paper and paste can be as permanent as the other components of a book and since paste is perfectly satisfactory as an adhesive, there is little or no need for modifications in Cockerell's procedure, in so far as the use of modern material is concerned. Where specially strong guards are required—as, for example, the linen guards for reinforcing the sewn joint of end papers—the most perfect material is, perhaps, the fabric from which the war escape maps were made. It consisted of a nylon base very heavily sized with some waterproof material. This fabric was very thin and extremely strong. It could not be satisfactorily stuck down with paste and called for P.V.A. emulsion; such a joint, when well made, is extremely strong and thin enough to be almost invisible. If this material cannot now be obtained a good substitute can be made from fine cambric soaked in 15 per cent gelatine solution and dried and pressed flat. This also justifies the use of P.V.A. emulsion and produces a strong unobtrusive reinforcement.

The guarding of vellum leaves is an operation which might well be done with P.V.A. emulsion. Ordinary paste between vellum gives a joint somewhat weaker than vellum, and P.V.A. is better in this respect; if a well-made joint is pulled apart it comes away with some of the vellum surface attached to the break. At the same time, it must be borne in mind that vellum absorbs moisture much more freely than P.V.A. and, consequently, in a moist atmosphere, may expand much more to the point where the P.V.A. causes cockling or wrinkling of the joint. With two vellum sheets, however, the P.V.A. is the centre of a sandwich and this is perhaps the most satisfactory arrangement of the two types of material.

HINGE GUARDING

This method of binding sections uses a guard of the same thickness as the section; it is attached to the back of the section by sewing. The sewn joint provides a hinge and gives flexibility to the leaves of a section, even when this is made of paper so stiff as to give a book which would open badly when bound by the ordinary methods. This method has certain other advantages which recommend it very strongly. The sections are practically undamaged by the binding and can be released by cutting the sewing thread at the inner pages of the section. They can also be rebound without the trouble of guarding, knocking flat or the necessity of making repairs to the back of the section.

However, as almost the whole of the bending of the leaves of the section during use occurs at the sewn joint, the thread is very severely stressed and may fray and break. The durability of this type of binding depends largely on the use of a very strong flexible thread which will resist these repeated bending stresses for the normal life of the book. Linen thread seems scarcely strong enough but the newer synthetic fibres appear to be excellent for the purpose. They have immense strength and, when stressed, give the impression of the springiness of hard metal wire; this promises extremely good resistance to repeated bending.

The chief difficulty of these threads (as well as of silk which is almost as strong) is that they are built up of a large number of fine continuous filaments which are generally not very tightly twisted. Consequently, the individual filaments are inclined to separate during sewing and the thread thereby loses its coherence as an assemblage. If the load is thrown on individual fibres the great strength of the combination is lost. All these disadvantages can be overcome by soaking the thread in loose hanks in P.V.A. emulsion, diluted with water to about three times its original volume. On drying, the filaments composing the thread will all be lightly stuck together and it can be used without fear of fraying or unstranding.

The hinged guard can be made by wrapping paper round a thin strip of steel, about ½ in. wide and rather longer than the guard, until the requisite thickness has been attained (measured without the steel strip and pressed flat). When the paper is cut through at the side of the roll, the steel strip is released.

The exact thickness of these guards needs careful gauging; only experience can guide one as to the best thickness and the best method of measuring it in any particular case. If the pressed guard is slightly thinner than the fold of the section measured under the same conditions of pressure it will be about right in most cases. It is better to err on the side of too much thickness rather than too little, since guards which are too thin give the finished book an unpleasant gaping appearance.

When the back of a section has been repaired by using a straight-edged guard, the guarded leaf will tend to bend sharply at the line where the guard ends, especially if the paper of the section is soft or weak, and this will concentrate the stresses at that line and possibly cause the paper to crack and the leaf to become prematurely detached. For valuable books this threat to durability can be reduced by paring the edges of the guards. If this is not practicable a similar effect can be obtained by giving the guard scalloped edges, by for example, the use of the special scissors made for this purpose for dressmakers. Machine-made guards with scalloped edges are in use by the library-book repairer and, if not too wide and thick, are the cheapest and most convenient way of avoiding the risk of damage to the sharp edges of guards. They are, however, usually too thick for most fine work.

MENDING AND REPAIRING

The repair of books or papers which are to be permanent needs a different approach from the patching of library books to avoid the need for rebinding, and the faking of old and valuable books which is done to hide the repair from the purchaser. It is very doubtful if the newer materials already mentioned have any very marked advantage over the traditional materials. Most legitimate repairs will have reference to paper and, in such cases, it would be difficult to improve on the use of good quality hand-made paper and tissue and well-made paste.

Repairs to the binding will usually raise the question as to whether it would not be more satisfactory to rebind a damaged book in order to prevent such increased damage later that rebinding will then become urgent. Where minor damage, such as torn leather or other covering material, has to be repaired, the use of P.V.A. emulsion might well give a more satisfactory repair than paste or glue. Similarly, a damaged end paper might be repaired more satisfactorily with thin nylon fabric and P.V.A. emulsion than with more traditional materials.

Such small repairs may not justify rebinding and may often be carried out with modern threads, adhesives and fabrics. However, with a repair of this kind, it should never be forgotten that if materials of widely different character are to be used side by side their mutual incompatibility may manifest itself in warping, wrinkling or other ways which would not occur had the repair materials been similar to or compatible with the existing materials of the book.

The repair of vellum and parchment usually calls for a stronger adhesive than paste and, moreover, one which adheres to these materials. P.V.A. (polyvinyl acetate) emulsion is superior to glue or paste for this purpose.

CLEANING AND RE-SIZING

The pages of old books and old paper documents are sometimes disfigured by "foxmarks" and are quite often soft and spongy. Various procedures have been advocated from time to time for removing foxmarks and re-sizing. It cannot be too strongly emphasized that any chemical treatment violent enough to bleach a bad foxmark effectively will require the greatest care in application, even by the specialist, if the paper is not to be irreparably damaged.

The commonest of these remedies is to soak the paper in weak permanganate solution, to remove the brown manganese dioxide which is deposited in the paper, to wash in water and finally to re-size the paper. The first two operations are dangerous to paper unless carried out skilfully and the washing must be done much more thoroughly than is possible in the absence of suitable apparatus. These operations certainly remove the foxmarks and bleach the paper to a brilliant white. If correctly carried out, they leave the paper not appreciably damaged and, with adequate sizing, much stronger than before.

Treatments using hypochlorites or other active chlorine-containing substances should always be avoided as these are even more difficult to carry out safely than the permanganate treatment.

It should be borne in mind that the paper under a bad foxmark may be too brittle and rotten to stand any wet treatment. Re-sizing is best carried out with a warm 2–5 per cent solution of gelatine in warm water. If a slight brown colour is not objectionable, glue can be used in the place of gelatine and the solution need not then be kept warm, except in a cold workshop. Some archivists use a size prepared by boiling vellum cuttings in water until dissolved. The use of glue or gelatine ready prepared is much simpler and free from any risk of impermanence.

The safest way of treating foxmarks is to bathe the paper in a very weak alkaline solution made from water containing one-fifth of one per cent of washing soda. Plenty of solution should be used; often it will also remove some colour from discoloured papers and usually it will reduce the colour of the foxmarks, though not always to the point of complete bleaching.

When documents are to be silked the weakening effect of ultra-violet light on silk should be kept in mind; also the possibility of the transference of the weakness of the paper to the silk. Paper may have become brittle through the development of high acidity and unless this is washed out or neutralized before silking the silk may also become brittle. If the brittleness of the paper is due to mould growth, as in the case of foxing and brown rot, the damage might be communicated to the silk unless the size solution contains a fungicide. The methods of removing acid from paper have been mentioned previously (*see* p. 40). For the use of fungicides see page 37.

END PAPERS

These are rarely strong enough to withstand constant use over long periods and are usually the weakest part of a good binding. The use of leather joints is a doubtful advantage as regards permanence and strength. End papers made of a good-quality paper, with the sewn fold reinforced with thin cambric fabric fastened in place with P.V.A. emulsion, are satisfactory. There is something to be said for the uncommon practice of reinforcing the joints of the boards with one of the fine fabrics and, in this way, relieving a vulnerable part of the paper of much of the stress caused by the constant sharp bending which occurs with a close joint. If well-sized fabric is used, the end paper can be stuck down to it with paste in the usual way and if the fabric is thin enough its presence will not unduly interfere with the snug closing of the boards.

Whenever paper is likely to be incapable of standing up to severe bending or where it is to hold thread, the use of well-sized nylon fabric with P.V.A. emulsion is recommended. Such a combination is excellent as regards resistance to bending, tearing, flexibility and unobtrusiveness but it must always be remembered that a joint is only as strong as its weakest component, when nylon fabric and paper are joined together the paper is the weakest component and a joint so formed is unlikely to be much stronger than a pasted joint between paper.

The use of P.V.A. is, however, necessary when nylon is used since paste and glue cannot generally be relied upon to give good adhesion to the nylon and may then constitute the weakest component of the combination. The use of the nylon-P.V.A. combination as a substitute for the more conventional leather joint, and used in the same way, is well worth a trial, since it would be thin enough to be covered by the end paper. This would then be pasted down in the usual way, except that the joint at the edge of the boards would be reinforced under the paper.

ROUNDING AND BACKING

One of the most interesting and promising uses for the modern synthetic adhesive, P.V.A. emulsion, is in lining the spine of a book after backing. When dry, P.V.A. is rubbery and it remains so even after the prolonged heating of the accelerated ageing test. Minor risks only are attendant upon its use as the book can be rounded and backed in the orthodox manner and the P.V.A. used solely for lining. Whatever the lining material—brown paper, linen, leather or a synthetic fabric—P.V.A. can be relied upon to give an excellent bond between it and the back of the sections and its flexibility will allow of the use of much more solid lining material than will glue or paste.

If, however, the binder is prepared to take for granted the permanence of P.V.A., he can often dispense with the use of any other adhesive for rounding, backing and lining. A book fairly tightly sewn on cords can often be rounded by hand pressure more easily even than by the standard method and irregularities in the "round" can be more easily corrected in the dry state. If the rounded book is clamped between backing boards, the backing can usually be started on the dry spine by pushing over the sections with a piece of wood.

At this stage, the spine should be well moistened with water which should be allowed to soak into the paper, more being added if necessary to ensure even damping. If enough water is used and sufficient time allowed, the back of the sections becomes so soft that backing is very easily carried out by gentle persuasion from a piece of wood held in the hand. When the back has been shaped in this way, it may be hammered to consolidate the backs of the sections and to give them a slight "keystone" shape to ensure of a solid spine.

In most cases, it is advantageous to allow the spine to dry in the press, smoothing it from time to time during drying in order to prevent the formation of ridges corresponding to the backs of sections. If this ridging is not to be feared, the damp spine should be covered with P.V.A. emulsion and the lining material, also painted with P.V.A., applied and pressed well into contact with the back.

A piece of cinefilm, about one foot long and the correct width to go between the band or tapes and pulled down over the back, is handy for ensuring contact and preserving the shape of the spine. Once the lining is attached in this way it is not easy to alter the set of the back and this may be something of a disadvantage since cleaning off cannot readily be done. On the other hand, it is usually an advantage to have a back which holds its form tenaciously. If cleaning off is essential, rounding and backing should be carried out in the usual way and the P.V.A. used for lining only.

It is more difficult to undo what has been done with P.V.A. than it is with glue or paste. Should undoing be necessary (even the best craftsman can slip occasionally), the P.V.A. can be softened by heating it to about the temperature of boiling water, when it loses its adhesiveness. If it is to be cleaned from the back or other surface on which it has dried, solvents should be used. Methylated spirit will soften P.V.A. sufficiently to enable it to be scraped off with a blunt knife, while the lacquer solvents, such as acetone, ethyl acetate and butyl acetate, will work even more rapidly and completely. These solvents are all inflammable and readily ignite while non-inflammable solvents are usually somewhat anæsthetic and contain the chlorinated organic substances which, in connexion with bookbinding materials, should be used with great caution.

CUTTING EDGES

Cutting and treating the edges of a book call for little comment. The time-honoured edge gilding is still by far the most decorative and protective method of treatment. It is perhaps unfortunate that it requires great skill to carry it out effectively and this is the only reason for suggesting an alternative treatment. This consists in polishing the newly-cut edge, while still in the lying press, with a wax polish. A good-quality furniture wax (not the emulsion type) is quite satisfactory, provided it is not coloured. For anyone who wishes to try to make his own preparation, a mixture of equal parts of beeswax, carnauba and hard paraffin wax, dissolved in turpentine or white spirit by careful heating, will give satisfactory results.

The book edge is polished in the way used for furniture and may be burnished if desired. The effect is to give a slight polish to the edge and to make it appreciably water repellent. Furthermore, dust is less likely to adhere to such a surface than to an untreated edge. A still better finish can be obtained by scraping the edge before waxing.

COVERING

The use of leather for covering has received so much attention for generations that modern materials can add nothing of value to the process used by the old binders. Well-made paste appears to have all the properties desirable in an adhesive used for this purpose. So far, modern research can only help in providing a leather which will not perish in the modern atmospheres to which it is exposed. The use of other covering materials for sides has already been mentioned and here again the traditional adhesives, glue and paste, will hold their own. It may indeed be true that the use of P.V.A. or other semi-waterproof adhesive for the comparatively large surface of the boards to be covered will cause warping with changes in humidity and air temperature, whereas glue and paste will tend to follow the expansion and contraction of the boards and so be less liable to cause warping.

When, however, one departs from the traditional coverings and uses some of the newer synthetic materials, or even silk, P.V.A. may be necessary to give a good bond between these and the boards. Since the permanence of a book is less affected by the material used for covering the boards than by other materials, much greater latitude is permissible in the choice of material for this purpose. With quarter leather binding, the leather is mainly confined to the spine where its unique properties particularly fit it for good service, but the sides, which do not require a supple material, can be covered with a more wear-resisting material, one which will take the punishment usually meted out to the corners of the boards better than leather.

Such wear-resisting materials are vellum and tailor's canvas impregnated with hardened gelatine. When siding with this latter material, the board as well as the fabric, should be glued or pasted and the fabric applied and given a nip in the press and allowed to dry partially. The "turning in" can then be done very easily and neatly by pasting the projecting edges and, when soft, "turning in" and making them snug at the edges and corners with a folder. The boards should then be pressed between tins until all is firm and dry.

Then, and not before this stage, the gelatine should be hardened by swabbing the fabric with a 5 per cent solution of tannic acid in spirit. The swab should be just wet enough to moisten the fabric which dries in a few minutes without warping the boards. If the somewhat harsh feel of the fabric is disagreeable it should be swabbed with a 10 per cent solution of shellac in spirit and allowed to dry. This gives a smooth and pleasant handle to the sides and tones them a pleasing brown.

Some people claim that cutting tailor's canvas at 45° to the warp threads, gives a greatly improved appearance to the finished side and assists the binder to get a neatly finished "turn in" at the corners. Another very pleasant siding material can be made from tailor's canvas impregnated with either ethyl cellulose or cellulose acetate solution. No after treatment is needed for these materials but the purist may suspect their permanence.

BIBLIOGRAPHY

ASTLE, T., *The Origin and Progress of Writing* (London, 1803).

BARROW, W. J., *The Barrow Method* (State Library Building, Richmond, Virginia, U.S.A., 1954).

BAUER, J. V., *Use of Cereal Products in Adhesives*, **12**, pp. 252-7 (1954).

BLAGDEN, *Some Observations on Ancient Inks*, **77**, (ii), p. 451 (1787).

BRAUDE, FELIX, *Adhesives* (Chemical Publishing Co., Brooklyn, U.S.A., 1943).

BRIQUET, C. M., *Les Filigranes* (Geneva, 1907; Leipzig, 1923).

CLAPPERTON, R. H., *Modern Paper-Making* (Oxford, Basil Blackwell, 1952).

COCKERELL, D., *Bookbinding and the Care of Books* (London, Pitman, 1948).

COMPAÑÍA URUGUAYA DE FOMENTO INDUSTRIAL, S.A., *Ball-Point Inks*, B.P. No. 701,061.

DARD HUNTER, *Paper-Making Through Eighteen Centuries* (New York, William Edward Rudge, 1930).

DARD HUNTER, *Paper-Making* (New York, Alfred A. Knopf, 1943).

DE BRUYNE and HOUWINK, *Adhesion and Adhesives* (London and New York, Elsevier Publishing Co., 1951).

DESBOROUGH, W., *Duplicating and Copying Processes* (London, Pitman, 1930).

DUTTON MEIRIC, K., *Historical Sketch of Bookbinding as an Art* (The Holliston Mills Inc., Norwood, Mass., U.S.A., 1926).

GRANT, JULIUS, *Books and Documents* (London, Grafton and Co., 1937).

HARRISON, T., *Bookbinding Craft and Industry* (London, Pitman, 1926).

HEAWOOD, E., "The use of watermarks in dating old maps and documents," *Geogr. Journ.*, **63**, p. 391 (1924).

KIRK-OTHMER, *Insecticides* and *Fungicides. Paper Fillers* (New York, Interscience Encyclopaedias Inc., 1947).

LANGWELL, W. H., "Permanence of Paper," *Technical Bull. of Brit. Paper and Board Makers Assn. (Inc.)*, London, Vol. 29, pp. 21, 52 (1952), Vol. 30, p. 2 (1953). *Proc. Tech. Sect.*, B.P. and B.M.A., **36**, p. 199 (London, 1955).

LYDENBURG and ARCHER, *The Care and Repair of Books* (New York, 1945).

MARTIN and POTTER, *Ball-Point Inks*, B.P. No. 621,847.

MITCHELL, C. A., *Inks, Composition and Manufacture* (London, Griffin, 1937).

PLENDERLEITH, H. J., *The Preservation of Leather Bookbindings* (London, British Museum, 1947).

PLENDERLEITH, H. J., *The Conservation of Prints, Drawings and Maunscripts* (London, British Museum, 1937).

RASCH, R. H., "Accelerated Ageing Test for Paper," *Journal Research National Bureau of Standards*. Research Paper No. 352, **7**, p. 465 (1931).

SÉE, PIERRE, *Papier Piqué*. (Comptes Rendues Acad. Science, Paris, Vol. 164, p. 230 (1917)).

SÉE, PIERRE, *Les Maladies du Papier Piqué* (Paris, Dom et Fils, 1919).

SMITH, GEORGE, *Moulds and Tropical Warfare* (London, Endeavour, 1946).

SUTERMEISTER, EDWIN, *The Story of Paper-Making* (Boston, 1954).

INDEX

ACCELERATED ageing tests, 91
for inks, 48
for nylon and terylene, 59
Rasch, 21
for acidity of paper, 21
Acetic acid for liquid glue, 71
Acetone in the impregnation of paper, 39
Acid—
acetic for liquid glues, 71
danger to paper, 16, 17
difficulty of removing from paper, 16
effect on breakdown of cellulose, 14, 16
hydrochloric, action on paper, 27
hydrocyanic (prussic) for fumigation, 31
in inks, 47
in paper, effect of buffers, 22
in paper manufacture, 16
pastes, 66
weak, effect on paper, 17
Acidity—
of newsprint, 19
of paper,
measuring, 18
micro-tests, 36
most favourable, 16, 19
of sizes, 11
pH scale of, 18
Adhesion, general principles, 63
Adhesives—
alkaline, danger of, 15
blood albumen in, 69
effect on warping and wrinkling of paper, etc., 97
for rounding and backing, 99
mechanical damage to paper by, 63
modern synthetic, 74
setting and drying of, 63
Ageing—
effect on paper of natural, 13
of inks, 48
(see Accelerated ageing tests)

Air—
conditioning,
removal of excess humidity, 32
removal of sulphur dioxide, 22, 25
conditions, suitable for parchment and vellum, 45
effect on cellulose, 14, 15
Albumen (blood) for adhesives, 69
Alkali—
for removing fox marks from paper, 98
in adhesives, danger of, 15
in inks, 49
in paper to protect against atmospheric damage, 22
in pastes, 66
in straw boards, 16
Alkaline breakdown of paper and cellulose, 15
Alkalinity, high, in inks, 49
Alpha (see Esparto)
Alum—
in paper,
acidity due to, 18
in paste, 67
in tub size, 11
Ammonia in tobacco smoke, 25
Aniline dyes—
fastness of, 49
in inks, 46
Animal sizes for paper, 11
Antiseptics—
for paper, spray application of, 15
for paste, to prevent mouldiness, 67
Arabic, gum, 73
Archives—
administration, courses in, vi
danger to, 15
lamination of, xx
microfilming, xxi
preservation in Great Britain, v
raw materials for, xviii
Archivist, science for the, vii
Art papers, surface weakness of, 57

Ash, tobacco, effect on paper, 25
Atmospheric conditions—
  best for parchment and vellum, 45
  effect on lamination, 24
Atmospheric dampness—
  effect on paper, 15
  effect on parchment and vellum, 31
Atmospheric oxidation of cellulose, 14, 15
Atmospheric sulphur dioxide—
  damage due to, 21
  micro-test for, 22, 35
  prevention of damage due to, 40

BACKING and rounding, 99
  glue for, 70
  liquid glue for, 72
Bacteria, effect on cellulose and paper, 15
Ball-point inks, 49
Barrow, lamination of paper, 22, 23
Beating of paper—
  effect on papermaking fibres, 7, 11
  hollander first used, 3
  introduction of metals during, 11
  loading during, 11
  sizing during, 11
Bedford County Record Office, v
Binding materials, effect of acid on, 16
Binding quarter, 102
Black inks, permanence of, 52
Blagden, inks used in early manuscripts, 46
Bleach residues in paper, 20
Blood albumen, for adhesives, 69
Blue-black inks, 46
Bookbinding—
  boards, permanence of, 82
  covering materials, permanence, 83, 85, 86, 101
  indiarubber used for, 92
  leather,
    permanence, 84
    sulphur damage to, 15
  materials, effect of acid on, 16
  quarter binding, 102
  strengthened joints for, 98
  techniques, effect on permanence, 91
  unsewn (single sheet) binding, 74, 93

Books—
  quarter binding, 102
  repairing, 96
  treatment of edges, 101
  treatment with fungicides, 39
Breakdown of paper—
  by atmospheric sulphur dioxide, 15
  with age, 13
British gums for adhesives, 66
British Museum, laboratory techniques, 36
British Records Association, v
Brittleness of paper—
  caused by acids, 16
  simple creasing test, 17
Brown decay in paper, 26
Brown rot in paper, 26
Brushes—
  cleaning after using P.V.A. adhesives, 79
  handling glue, 77
Buckram, permanence of, for books, 85
Buffering agents for paper, 22

CALCIUM carbonate in Barrow process of lamination, 22
Cambric for guarding, 94
Carbolic acid (*see* Phenol)
Carbon—
  disulphide for fumigation against insects, 31
  in early iron-gall inks, 46
  inks,
    for parchment and vellum, 51
    history of, 46
  tetrachloride,
    anaesthetic properties, 29
    for fungicides, 29
  tissue,
    fastness of carbon copies to solvents, 53
    waxy inks for, 52, 54
Carboxymethylcellulose (C.M.C.)—
  for lamination of paper, 23
  for paste making, 68
Casein for adhesives, 69
Catalytic metals in paper and atmospheric damage, 21, 22
Causes of damage to paper, 20
Cellophane for lamination of paper, 24